Mr Wonderful

A play

James Robson

Samuel French — London
New York - Toronto - Hollywood

Please see page iv for further copyright information

MR WONDERFUL

First presented at Derby Playhouse, in association with
Stars and Angels Ltd, on 28th October, 1997, with the
folowing cast:

Eric	Willie Ross
Norma	Paula Wilcox
Phoebe	Ann Rye
Geoff Lazenby	Ian Lindsay
Lop Wink	Willie Ross

Directed by **Paul Rider**
Designed by **Chris Crosswell**
Lighting by **Jason Taylor**
Sound by **Andrew Elsegood**

CHARACTERS

Norma Green
Phoebe Green, her mother
Geoff Lazenby
Eric Box
Lop Wink
Drunk
Waiter

The parts of Eric Box, Lop Wink, Drunk and Waiter can
be played by the same actor

COMPOSITE SETTING

Fragment of Manchester Pub/Southport Hotel: Ubiquitous dado rail and wallpaper (different for Seaside) on a couple of flats. Repro table and two chairs. Boddington's beermats, ashtray. In the pub, there should be a sign indicating "TOILETS" in the background. In the Southport Hotel, a telephone is on the wall *us*.

Greens' House: A semi or bog-standard terrace. Hallway from the front door with a telephone on the side table, a mirror above it, fairly tasteless old carpet. Doors to the kitchen, front room and sitting-room. Through the front room door can be seen a bit of a couch (with wooden arms) and a tiled fireplace. Typical print above that. Cheap ornament on the mantel.

In the sitting-room Phoebe has taken to her bed. The room is almost filled by an old brass bed with a feather mattress etc. Phoebe spends most of the play in bed and has been in situ for years, surrounded by knitting patterns, needles, wool, a tray with liquorice allsorts on it, women's magazines, Mills & Boon paperbacks, books about "Our Wonderful Royal Family". A telephone is on the bedside chair. A chamberpot is beneath the bed, and balls of dust. Her Zimmer frame is somewhere. A small bedside locker with pills and medicines, a water jug and a glass, a small portable TV (screen OOV), a framed photo of the Queen Mother smiling dottily in a pink hat. A picture of the Royal Family circa 1950s on the wall. A photo of Norma as a young girl. A photo of Phoebe cuddling the eponymous bear on a seat in the back yard circa 1930s. A photo of Arthur Green. Beside Phoebe throughout, lolling on a mound of pillows is a large teddy bear, a silent observer of the play—maybe with a fraying bow tie and an expression of inscrutable ursine urban angst.

A space UL or UR, containing Lop Wink's mountain bike on blocks.

NB: A revolve was used in the first production.

CHARACTERS

Norma Green: Aged 45. Working-class Mancunian, intelligent and self-aware—but undeveloped. Still shapely and attractive brunette. A warm-hearted, slightly loud and sentimental, but nervous woman trying to rediscover the person she "left behind", by using a local dating agency. She is a virgin, sometimes soulful and melancholy and still—sometimes agitated, lustful, frustrated. When she is occasionally crude, it is the involuntary spilling over of repressed desire. She has an instinctive sense of personal morality: she will not demean herself by settling for less than true love. She works part-time in a factory and cares for her elderly invalid mother. She is perceptive, dry, flip, witty, responsive and sharp but also rather old-fashioned. Beneath her strong "front" she carries a desperate menopausal sense of wasted time. A dizzy "chatterbox" at times, at others she is deeply shy and preoccupied with her thoughts to the point of seeming absent-minded.

Thanks mainly to her mother she has lost a lot of self-esteem over the years and longs to love and be loved; for a "meeting of true minds". She has had an average number of relationships with men, but always turned away from final commitment. A loving, obedient "Daddy's girl" whilst her father lived—she now fears growing old and turning into her mother with whom she has an ambivalent relationship: more love than hate, but fraught much of the time. Has two recurring catch-phrases: "There you go, then" and "This is it".

Phoebe Green: Aged 65. A bedridden lady in the very early stages of Alzheimer's. Her long-term memory is excellent, lurid—her recall of recent events fading and muddled. She has an immensely strong will and instinct for survival. Basically a good-hearted but rather stupid, giddy, amoral woman—she can be charming, amusing, kind, but is manipulative and has her claws deeply embedded in the heart of her only child Norma (Elizabeth, Margaret, Anne). It was at her instigation Norma began replying to dating agency inserts in the local paper. A latter-day Mrs Bennet who lives vicariously on her daughter's experiences, she is terrified that Norma will one day find her "Mr Wonderful". She has two voices: working-class Mancunian rough and "Queen Mum" posh, which she uses to excruciating effect. Her "Queen Mum" mode is an obvious, deliberate device to deflect unpleasant realities and to infuriate Norma. Empire Loyalist, Royalty Worshipper, dizzy old

Slapper—she has a serious liquorice allsorts addiction and always keeps by her side a big battered Edwardian (Farnell) teddy bear, called Mr Wonderful, whom she has come to regard as confidant, friend, surrogate grandchild, alter ego and repository of emotions.

Geoff Lazenby: Aged 50. A retired English & PT Teacher, burly and still handsome in a slightly florid way. He is well-mannered, erudite, jokey, stylish, plausible: the answer to a middle-aged maiden's prayer? A divorcee with a grown-up but distant son, he plays his courting cards to perfection, but may not be the Mr Wonderful he seems. He is a born pedagogue whose only obvious fault is that he has an answer to everything ("A right knowledge box", as Phoebe calls him at first). In fact, his urbane demeanour conceals a massive ego, an overwhelming cynicism, maybe a savage heart…? He is a charming wolf stalking through the abundance of the sad dating agency world—shocking when he shows his true colours, but understandable too by the end.

Eric Box: Aged 45-50. Mind-numbing Mancunian bore. One of Norma's suitors from the agency. Owner of a DIY Emporium with an encyclopaedic knowledge of his wares. A monotonous wimpish eunuch whose banal witterings gradually betray an inner state of throbbing lust. Looks as if he hasn't a good screw in him—but talks a fantastic screw! Needs to be played with deadly seriousness, without a trace of tongue-in-cheek.

Lop Wink: Middle-aged cycling freak of Dutch extraction who cycles mysteriously between later scenes of Act I and arrives to meet Norma on a date, dressed in skin-tight lycra, helmet, etc. A clean-living fitness fanatic with a mind like a swept cell. A man who has absolutely nothing to say and keeps on saying it. A prudish *Health & Efficiency* type—or does a fanatical hobby entail more than just pounding around the Pennines on his zillion-geared mountain bike?

With **Drunk** in Pub and **Waiter** in Southport Hotel.

NB: The rôles of Eric Box, Lop Wink, Drunk, and Waiter can be played by the same actor.

SONGS

In the Black-outs between selected scenes, a selection of songs from *The Best of Peggy Lee* should be played— some of these to play over the spectacle of Lop Wink, the mad cyclist, hurtling at a standstill towards his date with Norma.

Title song: *Mr Wonderful* sung by Peggy Lee. Words and Music by Jerry Block, Larry Hockener and George Weiss.

J. R.

Other plays by James Robson
published by Samuel French Ltd

Beulah

Falling Short

Mail Order Bride

ACT I

Scene 1

A Manchester pub. Night

Busy bar sounds in the background, with the jukebox playing Stand by Your Man *by Tammy Wynette*

Eric Box sits primly at a table, staring straight ahead

There are drinks on the table, empty tonic bottles. A moment passes. Box slowly regards the empty chair beside him and licks his lips

Norma enters from the toilets and approaches

Box stares into the distance again, as she sits down. She smiles wanly at his profile

Norma Sorry about that. Nerves, I think. Sometimes think I might as well chuck my drinks straight on the floor—cut out the middle man.

Box stares, unblinking

Or middle woman. As the case may be. Or middle person these days I suppose. On the trot all night sometimes I am. Could understand it if I'd had ten kids or something... (*She stops herself talking*) Listen to me chattering on. Always been a chatterbox, my mother says...
Box Where was I, Miss Green?
Norma Have you moved?
Box I meant—what was I talking about?
Norma Screws.
Box Ah yes, the humble screw...

Norma stares at him, eyes widening

Totally superior to the nail, of course. Nails are primitive. I imagine Noah used wooden nails, pegs and dovetail joints... What would he have given for a box of three inch screws?

Norma stares glassily and smiles when he glances at her

Nails crudely penetrate. After a while the wood "gives" around a nail and cohesion is lost… Technically speaking, only the head of a nail holds it in—but a screw… A screw has a thread and insinuates itself remorselessly into the body of the host… It bites deep, Miss Green—bonding with the host material, do you understand?

Norma There you go, then.

Box A steel screw will rust away before it relaxes its grip, Miss Green…

Norma This is it.

Box Screws are faithful unto death. They do not let go. Unregarded, unnoticed, but holding the fabric of society together. (*He looks around with some satisfaction*) Take away all the screws and this place would gently subside all around us.

She gives him a look, mortified, stunned

Brass screws, galvanised screws, copper screws, plastic screws—not my favourite—devils to count they are. (*He smiles smugly to himself*) Not that anyone counts screws in the Emporium—my staff weigh them unless it's just the odd dozen or so to put some shelves up—or a couple of screws for Lord knows what. Rabbit hutch door for the kids maybe. As you might expect, not many people ask for a single screw, Miss Green…

He regards her as she sips her drink, puts the empty glass down and stares dully ahead

Does happen though. On occasion. "A single screw, please", I have heard it said. We don't charge for a single screw, put it down to GCR, I say… (*He waits a moment, then goes on*) Good Customer Relations. But you do wonder. Not that many applications for a single screw. Its uses are manifold but limited. The solitary screw… (*Still staring sideways at her, he licks his lips*) I don't suppose a woman like you gives much thought to the common or garden screw, Miss Green, let alone the solitary screw…?

She half-smiles into the distance: don't you believe it

Women do not in my experience. Women are not my best customers. DIY remains something of a male preserve—though things are gradually changing. We do accommodate the odd woman in a boiler suit wanting a tool…

Norma blinks

Spanner... Set of chisels...

Norma There you go, then.

Box There's a screw factory in Oldham, Miss Green. I'd love to show you it. Used to be an annual event—the screw factory outing. It's a family firm, you see. But the young ones aren't interested any more. I've stopped putting up the list. They write "Mickey Mouse" etcetera on it... Last year only Miss Earnshaw from Accounts and myself went... It's a colossal building, Miss... May I call you Norma?

Norma Why not? (*She glances at her watch*) We go back all of half an hour.

Box Norma... The screw machines never stop. They are just—beautiful. You can talk about your Picassos and Van Goghs, but I regard the screw machines as works of genius too. They resemble lathes, Norma... Lathes— I like to say that word—it makes you do a squiggle with your tongue inside your mouth... Lathes... Lengths...

She senses he's slightly aroused, frowning a little

They stand in rows in white-washed halls, Norma... Only they're not lathes, they're screw machines—day and night they're fed with lengths of metal... Automatically, from hoppers. It's all computerised now, like everything else—hour after hour the programme goes on, almost unsupervised—the hoppers lift and the gleaming lengths of brass or copper or steel roll onto the feeders and are slid into the cogs, into the threading bits—and the screws drop gently, silently, filmed with oil, into the screw containers at the other end. You do wonder what mind invented such perfection, Norman—*I* do.

Norma This is it.

Box Some nights when I can't sleep I think of those machines. Lying in my single bed above the Emporium with the occasional car headlight fanning across the ceiling—I am calmed thinking of those screw machines... Great metal worms inching the rods through their bellies... In that temple of the screw in Oldham, Norma. Unceasingly productive... Potent... Perfect... (*His nearest hand starts a slow journey across the table top towards Norma's*)

She watches his hand without moving her head—in fascinated horror

Only the console lights changing as the programme runs. Length after slick length in the semi-darkness. The glow of the surrounding city on the long sky lights above. Length after length sliding into the lubricated teeth of the machines, slipping in, sliding in, fitting through—changing—screw after perfect screw dropping from the nether regions. And they say machines have no intelligence, Norma—no beauty, no sensuality, no soul. (*He moves his fingers towards hers*)

Norma (*just before his fingers reach hers*) Could I have another drink—
Eric?

He stops, suddenly annoyed, withdrawing his hand

Box Another drink.
Norma I'll get them if you like…
Box Never let it be said Eric Box doesn't know how to treat a lady! (*He picks
up her glass and stands*) Same again.

Norma nods

Norma If that's all right?
Box Of course. Good heavens I think the firm of Albert Box and Son can run
to another vodka and tonic! Have whatever you like, have a change—
"woman's prerogative" my mother used to say…
Norma Do they do Screwdrivers?

He looks blank then laughs rather hysterically and not really amused

Box Oh, very good! "Screwdrivers"—well I said I wanted a lady with a sense
of humour, didn't I! "Sense of humour essential", that's what I said.
Norma (*deadpan*) There you go, then.
Box Laughter. Good for the soul. Sound of a woman's laughter in the next
room—I miss that.
Norma You've been married, then, Eric?
Box Oh, no, I meant—my mother's… (*He is touched by a shade, then gets
a grip*) Rightie ho then, a solitary Screwdriver if possible—orft I go!

Box goes off R with a spring in his step

Norma considers for a moment

Norma (*softly*) "Orft I go"…? (*She shakes her head, picks up her handbag,
stands, and glances in the direction taken by Box*)

Norma goes off past the "Toilets" sign

A moment later Box comes back on

Box Norma, I'm afraid they don't do… (*Stopped by her absence he finishes
off sadly*) Screwdrivers.

Black-out

SCENE 2

Phoebe's room. About an hour later

The Lights come up on Phoebe sitting up in bed with her teddy bear beside her, leafing in a bored manner through a copy of Hello *magazine. She has liquorice allsorts on a tray on her lap and chews as she sings absent-mindedly a few lines from* Mr Wonderful. *She tosses the magazine aside and cuddles the bear, staring at the TV picture. She stops singing and pores over the liquorice allsorts*

Can I tempt you to a lickerarse log, Mr Wonderful?

She shakes the teddy's head, holding it from behind

Oh, fussy pants, are we? I suppose you want a coconut wheel or a lickerarse sandwich—well, I'm sorry… (*She pops a coconut wheel into her mouth*) Now I feel really mean, oh, go on… (*She put a colourful sweet to the teddy's stitched mouth and makes "clapping" chewing noises. In what she thinks is a little ursine voice, she growls*) Thank you, Mummy… (*She looks depressed suddenly and sighs over the tray*) Almost down to lickerarse logs again, Mr Wonderful… That's life for you… All the pretty ones get snapped up—all the colourful ones go and what are you left with… (*She pauses*) Have to chuck 'em out the window before Madam gets back… Soon be a lickerarse plantation out there…

She stops as she hears someone unlock the front door

Norma enters

Norma switches the light on in the hallway, puts her handbag on the side table, and regards herself in the mirror. She gives her reflection a wry "thumbs down", then comes along the hall

Norma (*calling*) Normal Norma calling the Mad Mullah—want a drink?

Phoebe overturns the tray, tosses the bear over the front end of the bed, and flops back on the pillows like a corpse. Norma listens a moment, then goes to the sitting-room door. Just before she enters the room, Phoebe opens her mouth wide and keeps it horribly agape

Halloo… (*She spots the bear and picks it up*) What you doing out of bed, Mr Wonderful? (*She stares over the brass bars at Phoebe*) Oh God.

Pause

Cuddling the bear, Norma does a little dance of joy

Oh God, thank you! Oh, you've taken the old bat at last! Oh, I'm going to start going to church, honest I am—oh *yes*! (*In an instant she is deadpan again, tosses the bear on to the bed. Pleasantly*) Shut it, Mother, you look like a cement mixer.

Phoebe obeys and sits up, furious

Phoebe Yes, madam! That's what you think you'll say, but one night those calloused words will choke you!

Norma grins, regarding her mother with folded arms

Norma Told you, I'll throw a street party.
Phoebe You don't know what you've got coming to you, my lass! I might see you out!

Norma sits on the bed and idly flips through the Hello *magazine*

Norma You'll pull that stunt once too often. The Grim Reaper'll say "That's enough, Phoebe Green", and whack you off by the stocking tops.

Pause

Norma relents, smiling at Phoebe

Been all right, have you?
Phoebe (*sulking*) I'm reading that—don't miss my place…
Norma Want a nice wash…?
Phoebe No, I don't!
Norma Comb your hair, make you sleep?
Phoebe No, I'm full of wind.
Norma It's the liquorice allsorts. You'll explode one day and redecorate the room.

Phoebe grabs the magazine from her and pretends to read it—face averted, sulking. Norma starts putting sweets back on the tray

Nothing but liquorice logs again I see…
Phoebe You have 'em, they're as black as your heart.
Norma Want a nightcap?
Phoebe (*awfully posh*) Noew, I *dewn't* thenk so…

Norma Oh, heck, not slipping into Queen Mum mode, are we? Haven't heard from her for ages.
Phoebe (*cuddling the bear*) What is the silly girl talking about, Mr Wonderful? Last thing we want is some smelly old Horlicks.

Norma gets up and heads for the door

Norma I'll be off then, work in the morning. Nighty night, Mummy dear—night, Strawballs.
Phoebe Don't call him that! I don't want a drink, that's all—is it a crime?
Norma You do, but you're being silly.

They glare at each other

(*Giving in a little*) Aren't you going to ask me how I got on?

Phoebe shakes her head bitterly. Norma moves again. As Norma reaches the door, Phoebe speaks

Phoebe How did you get on?

Norma grins at the door, then, straight-faced and forgiving, returns to sit on the bed

(*Reading from the paper*) "Mister Understanding seeks Miss Understood for outings, conversation and general do-it-togetherness—good listener, own business"... *What was he like?*
Norma Fantastic.
Phoebe Really, our Norma?
Norma He was a hunk...
Phoebe Go on. Sounded dry as dust on his tape, sounded oldish.
Norma Oh, he was mature, in the best sense of the word...
Phoebe Like Victor Mature? I loved Victor Mature—he was the antithetical of your father.
Norma He was a very distinguished man.

Phoebe giggles and cuddles the bear

Phoebe Hear that, Mr Wonderful? Distinguished, mature, got his own business. Did you go on somewhere from the Victoria Hotel?
Norma (*shrugging*) Asked me back to his penthouse flat above the business, but I thought, steady girl—play it cool.
Phoebe Did he speak nicely?

Norma Larry Olivier to the life. We talked about the theatre, art—he reckons
he's got a little Hockney in his bedroom.

Phoebe (*cluelessly*) Has he now. You should have asked to see it, our Norma.

Norma On the first date, on my own? You know the agency doesn't
recommend that…

Norma is having difficulty not laughing and Phoebe sees it

Phoebe You're having me on!

Norma As *if*…

Phoebe When are you seeing him again, then?

Norma Hard to say, he travels the globe on business.

Phoebe It's your attitude.

Norma What is?

Phoebe Why you never click.

Norma I haven't got an attitude.

Phoebe Yes, you have—you're sardinic.

Norma I'm not, whatever it means—anyway, I do click sometimes.

Phoebe Not for long, *never* for good…

Norma I'm not clicking for clicking's sake…

Phoebe You've nearly been through the paper—never seen any of 'em more
than twice. You think you're it.

Norma There was Milton—I went out with him three times.

Phoebe What was wrong with him? Why did you ditch him? He had lovely
manicured hands…

Norma Third date was at the pictures: *Bridges of Madison County*… Took
him an hour to put one of his lovely hands round my shoulders—then he
whispered "I've got something for you, love" and slid this long warm thing
into my hand. I went hot and cold.

Phoebe What thing?

Norma Tube of Rowntree's Gums. I sensed a certain lack of imagination in
Milton.

Phoebe You take some pleasing, madam.

Norma I'm selective.

Phoebe Fussy little madam! What about that Clive with the funny nose?

Norma He sniffed all the time.

Phoebe Sniffed? So what?

Norma I used to sit waiting for the next one. It really got up my nose—and
he pulled his knuckles till they popped. I can't do with mannerisms—
Henry had mannerisms, remember?

Phoebe Course I remember Henry. You could have had him—you were
engaged to him! (*She looks confused, thinking hard*) What happened to
him?

Norma We split up.
Phoebe Yes! A week before the wedding! You were standing on the table
in your wedding dress, getting the hem altered and you said: (*Like Norma*)
"I can't go through with it, Mother"—I stuck a pin into my finger and bled
on the invitations. He had his own house!
Norma He had his own noises, slurping his tea...
Phoebe Did I drop you on your head at some point? You're mad, our Norma.
Norma He was mad on oranges. Four pounds of Jaffas a week he got
through. We watched telly a lot and I used to dread him reaching for the
first one: "Think I'll have a Jaffa, love". He'd take out his Swiss Army
knife, you know—everything from a parmesan grater to an abortion kit on
it? He'd cut the peel off in perfect diamond shapes and pile them on the arm
of the couch. Then he'd separate the segments and line them up. Like
condemned prisoners, I used to think, like a little doomed queue for the
awful chamber of his mouth. Then he'd eat them... (*She masticates
solemnly, slowly and noisily*) Clap, clap, clap—each segment seemed to
last a lifetime... I couldn't face that! I could see those segments spanning
out the rest of my life.

Phoebe stares at her and shakes her head

Phoebe I think I'd do better than you at this dating lark—I don't think you
like men.
Norma Unlike your dear self, Mummy...
Phoebe Not my fault I was popular...
Norma Want me to fix you up? "Charming widow seeks Victor Mature
lookalike for rampant sex. Has own bed, liquorice allsorts and— (*she
punches the bear lightly*) furry sex toy"...

Phoebe pulls the bear away and cuddles him childishly

Phoebe Yarch— (*she makes a face*) I don't want any more men. I'd rather
have a box of liquorice allsorts.
Norma Or a tube of fruit gums?

*They laugh together. Norma moves on to the bed until her head is resting
beside Phoebe's lap*

Phoebe It does leave you—you know? The need...
Norma That's what I'm worried about.
Phoebe Anyway, I've got *my* Mr Wonderful...
Norma Best relationship you've ever had, Mummy dear.
Phoebe Relationship? What is that? Your dad and me didn't have one of
those. We just loved each other...

Norma rests her head on Phoebe's lap and holds one of her hands. She draws up her legs like a girl

Norma I'm tired.
Phoebe (*stroking her fringe*) I'll pick you out another date while you're at work. You've got to click sometime—it's the law of beverages...
Norma Not sure I want to go on. There's something just a bit—humiliating about it after a while. It's like joining a club full of people you wouldn't let join your club—if you had one.
Phoebe Stuck-up little madam, you are. If you couldn't have the best, you'd do without. I don't know where you got such airs and graces.
Norma (*drowsily*) They're all Desperate Dans and Lonely Lils.
Phoebe Don't see why you can't just go out to a dance and meet something in trousers normally.
Norma S'not that easy these days.
Phoebe I met your dad on a foursome set up by a mate of mine. Alice Smith, by heck she was hot stuff—we met these two lads outside the Odeon. "This is my pal Phoebe Greaves", Alice said to your dad. Later on he said, "Funny name Verdigris intit?" He was full of jokes, your dad. What is verdigris, our Norma?
Norma Haven't a clue.
Phoebe We clicked straight away. He walked me right to the front step though it was miles out of his way.
Norma Have a knee-trembler in' door oil, did yer?
Phoebe (*oblivious, remembering*) I gave him my hand to shake, and he kissed it instead and went swaggering off with cig' smoke wafting over his shoulders.
Norma Bet you didn't wash it for days...
Phoebe I knew we'd clicked and no mistake. I ran up to bed but couldn't sleep for excitement. I lay there going over everything we'd said and done.
Norma (*sleepily*) As you do.
Phoebe His name was lit up in lights in my head.
Norma Arthur Green.
Phoebe This man you met tonight, our Norma... Give him another chance? Nobody's perfect, you know.
Norma 'Cept Mr Wonderful.
Phoebe You could do a lot worse than a man with a DIY Emporium.
Norma (*almost gone*) I wouldn't touch him with oven gloves on. Screw him... (*She is asleep, breathing heavily, relaxed with her head on Phoebe's lap*)

Phoebe stares down at her daughter's face with an expression of love tinged with anxiety—with the pain of loving. A moment of unspoken tenderness

Black-out

A recording of Peggy Lee singing My Heart Belongs to Daddy *begins to play*

SCENE 3

Phoebe's room. The following Saturday night

The room is bathed in an early evening glow

Norma, dressed for another date, is checking her make-up in the dressing table mirror

Phoebe is reading a paper in bed

Phoebe Here's a new recruit... "Needs emotional rescue and unconditional love... Tall, very bright gentleman living on the coast"...
Norma Sounds like a lighthouse.
Phoebe What about this, then——
Norma (*interrupting*) I've got a date for tonight.

Phoebe pulls a face and makes a disgusted noise

Now what?
Phoebe "Bubbly bisexual lady seeks bilingual lover for worldwide travel and cunningual—cunnilingual comradeship"—some people have got to have the lot, haven't they!
Norma Keep out of the Alternative Column—if it starts with "Straight" read on... (*She turns and regards her mother*)
Phoebe "Sensitive elderly Jack Russell seeks lady friend for walks in Dales"—is this the "Pets Connect" column?
Norma Savva look... (*She goes to the bedside and peers inside the paper held by Phoebe*)
Phoebe Some of these people should be *dis*-connected, if you ask me.
Norma (*reading*) "Sensitive, *comma*, elderly, *comma*—Jack Russell by name and a wag by nature"—God save us...
Phoebe Some of these people want locking up...

Norma moves away from the bed and turns

Norma Do I look OK?

Phoebe scrutinises her

Phoebe Don't sit under a strong light.

Norma sticks her tongue out then heads for the door

You be careful, our Norma, remember the agency guidelines.

Norma (*stopping*) Don't say that to me every time. You put me up to this.

Phoebe I want to see you provided for—I'm not immoral and I don't want you to be alone for the rest of your life.

Norma Immor*tal*.

Phoebe Tate and Lyle sugar you are: "Untouched by human hand"…

Norma (*hit, staring*) Don't keep saying that… I hate it when you say that.

Phoebe (*picking up the hand mirror and studying her reflection*) Speak truth, shame Devil…

Norma There's nothing wrong with celibacy. Lots of people are choosing it these days.

Phoebe (*pouting and primping at her reflection*) These days are barmy. Where would you be if I'd stayed Tate and Lyle?

Norma shakes her head ruefully

You should think on. As a woman you start to go invisible around forty— nobody listens to you or notices what you look like any more. (*She sighs*) I'm transparent now, soon I'll be invisible—I'll look in this mirror and I won't be there.

Norma Don't talk so daft.

Phoebe You're not drinking in the Last Chance Saloon any more, our Norma—you're standing in the road outside—in heavy traffic.

Norma drifts to the dressing table and looks at herself in the mirror

Norma Left it too late. Is that what you're trying to tell me?

Phoebe puts the mirror down and picks up the paper

Phoebe You've still got your own teeth.

Norma Thanks, Mummy dear.

Phoebe (*reading the paper*) Some of these sound more promising…

Norma (*moving back to the bed*) You've got to read between the lines—get the shorthand, the code? Most of 'em are downright hopeless for a start…

Phoebe What you on about? Honest, our Norma, you'd make trouble in an empty house!

Norma sits beside her and scans the columns

Norma Right. "Mature" means he's got both sets, wears incontinence pants
and arthritis bracelet... "Sexy guy" is a *Sun* reader who tosses off to
Baywatch.

Phoebe Our Norma! No need to be crude...

Norma "Cultured"? Watches Mastermind occasionally and collects Wade
Whimsies... "Wild child" keeps exotic pets in the bathroom and has taught
his budgie to say "Get your knickers off". "Slightly chubby cheerful
chap"? He's twenty stone and would laugh if his Y-fronts were on fire.
"Traditional male with similar views"? Middle-aged skinhead with stitches
tattooed around his neck.

Phoebe (*cutting in*) Well, you should know! You've been with most of
them...

Norma I'm just telling you what it's like out there.

Phoebe Don't go then! I don't mind—we'll send for a pizza and do a jigsaw
like we used to.

Norma considers this for a moment

Norma One more time, Mummy dear—then I'm all yours.

Phoebe I worry about you when you're out, you know? I miss you.

Norma stops and kisses her cheek

Norma There you go then.

Phoebe I don't know where all these weirdos are coming from. People used
to be sensible.

Norma turns towards the door

So who's the lucky man tonight, then? One of them serial killers?

Norma Don't even joke about it. (*She heads for the door*)

Phoebe (*her mood swinging*) Don't worry, your attitude would scare Boris
Karloff off... One of your looks could wither any man...

Norma stops between the bed and the door

Norma Anything else? Just to make me feel really good about myself before
I go?

Phoebe Word of advice...

Norma (*turning, mock incredulous*) Word of advice? After all these years?
Not sure I'm ready for this, Mummy dear.

Phoebe Don't gush.

Norma (*sighing*) I do not gush.

Phoebe And don't chatter.

Norma controls herself

Always been a chatterbox. I had to go to school about you once—disrupting classes. If this one is anything like—try not to chatter at him like a demented chimpanzee?

Norma heads briskly for the door

Norma Got everything you need, good—see you later!
Phoebe Who is it tonight?
Norma You picked him out.
Phoebe Well, it's just slipped my mind! Which one? You're supposed to tell someone where you're going and who with!

Norma returns to the bed and picks up the telephone

What are you doing? I don't want to talk to him!
Norma Voice mailbox, Mummy—I've explained it over and over again. (*She dials her number and listens*)
Phoebe Voice mailbox! What about lovely love letters? What about all the postmen?
Norma Connected... (*She puts the receiver into Phoebe's hands*) Pick the bones out of that. (*She exits along the hallway, gives the customary "thumbs up" to the reflection in the hall mirror, grinning*) Listen, you are drop-dead-roll-me-over-an-do-it-again-bells on your *nipples-gorgeous*, OK? (*Her shoulders sink, she loses her grin. Wryly*) Yeah, I know, love, give us a break.

Norma goes out and locks the door

In the sitting-room, Phoebe listens, wide-eyed, to the voice mailbox

Lazenby (*on tape*) I hesitate to describe myself as cultured. Not completely sure what that means anyway, but I do read omnivorously—autobiographies, biographies, slightly obscure novels *not* on the Booker List. I'm divorced, might as well get that out of the way—amicably enough, thank God. Afraid I'm not terribly good at this, not keen on talking to *things*—much better at kids, dogs, people, ladies of course, though I'm rather shy. So... Oh, dear, mind's gone blank again. Oh, I've got a stylish old banger I like to whizz over the Pennines in now and then, so if you can't stand having your hair blown all over the shop—don't apply. Let's sum it up, shall we: cultured, scholarly, fifty-something gentleman. Early retired and physically built for comfort and pleasure rather than speed! Rather like my car! Seeks companion of t' other gender for theatre, conversation, films, walks, and drives in aforesaid old banger. (*He chuckles pleasantly*)

Phoebe coos and squeaks

Non-smoker preferred as I've managed to chuck the weed myself, but bad habits include singing Sinatra in the bath and reciting the odd Shakespearian sonnet! So, if that hasn't entirely put you off, why not ring me on...

Phoebe puts the receiver to the bear's ear, in a tizzy of excitement

Phoebe Oouuh! I *say*...

Black-out

A recording of Peggy Lee singing Somebody Loves Me *plays*

SCENE 4

The pub. About 8 pm, the same night

A jukebox is playing an Oasis *number faintly in the background*

Norma is seated in the same chair, with a drink in front of her

She looks up as a well-dressed drunk weaves into view from L

She regards him with some trepidation: is this the date? The drunk leans carefully on the edge of the table with his knuckles and produces a long but totally unintelligible string of gibberish, which ends with a rising querying inflection

Drunk Aurghaurghuachaughuaghorchaugh?
Norma (*calmly*) Listen, mate, I'll get my tits out when you plonk your wizened little bits and pieces on the table—OK?

The drunk grunts with disappointment

Drunk I'll take that as a "No", then?
Norma Nothing's for nothing in this life, mate.

The drunk weaves off towards the "Toilets" sign and exits

Norma checks her watch and looks fed-up. She drains her glass and picks up her handbag, ready to leave

Lazenby approaches from R, *half a pint of beer in his hand*

Lazenby Hallo.

She looks up at him as if she hadn't seen him coming, and smiles politely

Are you…?
Norma Norma Green. Well, Norma Elizabeth Margaret Anne Green actually, but Norma will do for now, never use the others, never tell anyone they're there, in fact—Elizabeth, Margaret and Anne have had a very easy time of it so far, you might say—listen to me chattering on, you must be thinking "What have I unleashed"? Well, I'll shut up in a minute—Norma Green will be fine for now. Sounds like a disease I always think. "I've got Norma Green". Oh God, I am sorry, but if you will go on these long-haul holidays, never mind, I've heard it's not as bad as gangrene…

She stops as Lazenby reaches out a hand. She touches his fingers with hers and nods

How d'you do. Isn't that a strange thing to say? How d'you do what? Put your tights on in the morning?
Lazenby I was in the Saloon Bar, didn't know Cocktail Lounges still existed. (*He looks around, not impressed*)
Norma Oh yeah, just don't serve cocktails any more. No use asking for a Screwdriver in here—or a bag of Spanners come to that.

He regards her, smiling gently, relaxed

Sit if you like, it's the same price as standing.

He sits and regards her. She feels compelled to fill the pause

Green's not the best surname to have.
Lazenby Guisseppe Verdi did rather nicely on it…
Norma (*with a blank look*) "Cabbagelugs" they used to call me at school till I joined the judo class. "Eat up your greens, Cabbagelugs" they used to say at dinners—sorry… Chattering mode comes on under stress.
Lazenby There's nothing wrong with your name, Norma.
Norma (*making a face*) No? You just said it and I got a sinking feeling.
Lazenby Norma…

She slumps slightly in her chair

Norma Norma. This is it. First time I heard John Major's wife was called Norma, I felt like topping myself—then I saw her… Every time I saw him after that—peering out of the telly like an old maid with piles—I used to think, "Where's *Norma*"? Where's my namesake and does she have any idea what pain she's causing me? What's she doing today? Is she shopping? Knitting a nice jumper for John? (*In a John Major voice*) "Norma, I *went* a jumper!"

She realizes he's smiling and checks herself

I don't always go on like this—well, I do quite a bit, Mother's right—I hear myself, you know, but I can't stop it—it's like sitting inside this runaway bus—God, when I get going—"Got with a gramophone needle" my father used to say. (*She stops*)

He smiles kindly at her. She makes an aside to the ceiling

Shut *up*, mad cow. Stop gibbering… (*She looks at him like a ventriloquist with her face rigid, jaws clamped shut*)
Lazenby I'm Geoff Lazenby by the way.
Norma (*almost venting*) Nothing wrong with that name.
Lazenby Boring old name, like its owner. Sounds like a firm of glaziers, I always think.

Pause

Well, here we are then.
Norma This is it.

Pause

Lazenby ⎫ (*together*) ⎧ You got here OK?
Norma   ⎭   ⎩ You got here all right, then?

He laughs. She smiles

Lazenby After you.
Norma You got here all right, then.

He nods urbanely, amused

In the stylish old banger, I presume?

She winces at her own words, then bristles a bit as he just nods his head and smiles, waits for more gaffes, and nods

You do speak of your own accord? I feel like Big Ears chatting up Noddy here.

He laughs delightedly. She smiles broadly, lighting up the space. The ice splinters

Lazenby Sorry. I try to engage the old grey matter before opening my mouth…
Norma Meaning I don't?
Lazenby No, no—look, early cards on table, OK?
Norma (*shrugging*) There are worse things.
Lazenby (*looking puzzled but going on*) I think you are delightful, fascinating—that's why I'm just… Taking you in.

She stares at him, can this be true?

Norma Bit of a stylish old banger yourself, aren't you? I hope this isn't patronising bullshit.
Lazenby Please… Norma… I didn't mean it to sound like that. (*He looks downcast suddenly, sad, boyish*) Perhaps you know how it is. Hours on one's own with nothing but the radio or the cat to talk to, then suddenly… Someone… It's rather a bumpy transition—I'm sorry.

She looks more at ease and smiles at him

Can I get you a drink?
Norma All right for now, ta.

He looks away. She looks disgusted at herself

(*Murmuring in disbelief*) Ta?

They both look at each other again and go totally blank. He drums his fingers on the table and stops when she looks at them. She looks incredibly depressed, desperate

Lazenby This is bloody awful, I'm sorry…

She freezes in her chair, she simply goes dead; her face wipes itself into a coldly staring mask. He looks at her but she can't meet his eyes. Another paralysed moment, then she picks up her handbag

Norma Sorry to have wasted your time. There you go then, or should I say
   "Orft I bloody well go"...
Lazenby No, I meant—this dating business is awful.
Norma Needs must when the Devil drives... (*She stops and groans at the
   crassness of this utterance*)
Lazenby Haven't heard anyone say that for years.
Norma Never heard myself say it before actually.
Lazenby I feel quite useless in these situations. All the clever lines I've
   prepared go clean out of my head and... (*He stops and shrugs attractively*)
   You must think a right—chump.
Norma Haven't heard anyone say that for years.

He stares

   Chump?
Lazenby (*smiling*) *Touché.*
Norma *Never* heard anyone say that before.

He looks sad again, lost for words

   I know what you mean though—about the situation. It's a set-up, isn't it?
   Artificial...
Lazenby (*nodding gratefully*) It kills the subtlety, I think.
Norma I think Cardinal something or other said "*Touché*" a lot in *The Devil
   Rides Out* by Dennis Wheatley.
Lazenby He probably said: "Needs must when the Devil drives" too...

They laugh together

Pause

He sighs

   Meetings, eh... I met my wife, my ex-wife I should say—on a mountain
   in Crete—we were both on walking holidays—she'd pitched her tent
   across this track in the dark and I fell into it. She thought I was a Cretan
   shepherd on the make.
Norma (*downed*) Oh. Can't compete with that, I'm afraid...
Lazenby You're not competing with anything. We lived in hell for twenty-
   five years, then parted with surprising accord—and relief—we both said:
   "Why did we wait so long"?

Norma nods

When I said "This is awful" I meant—it does away with that delicacy some
people have when they meet and are immediately, naturally—attracted...
That "sensing" process...
Norma Had many dates, then?
Lazenby (*sticking up three fingers*) A few... (*He stares a reciprocal
question*)
Norma Same here.
Lazenby Dreadful, some of them, aren't they?
Norma Desperate.
Lazenby I mean, one doesn't like to be unkind...
Norma My mother says: "There's a lid for every pot"...

He laughs again. She smiles, happy to amuse

Pause

But some of 'em have been on fire too long.

He laughs, they relax a shade

Pause

Your description said "scholarly"...
Lazenby Yes, rather pompous, I know, but... I was a teacher, that's all. Took
early retirement. Walked out of those school gates like a released prisoner.
Norma Comprehensive?
Lazenby Grammar. (*He pauses*) English and PT.
Norma Physical Torture that meant to me. I'm not athletic in the accepted
sense of the word.

He laughs

Funny combination, wasn't it?
Lazenby (*deadpan*) The Greek ideal, Norma—perfection of body and mind?
Norma (*staring, serious*) There you go, then.
Lazenby I'm joking! I lord the fight to stay thin...
Norma (*regarding him*) I don't mind the odd love-handle.
Lazenby Love what?
Norma (*shaking her head*) Never mind.
Lazenby You've got a vocabulary all of your own, haven't you?
Norma This is it. I say funny things an' all.

He laughs

Started talking to myself lately— (*tongue obviously in cheek*) laughing at
my own jokes...
Lazenby But you have your mother...
Norma Oh, I talk to her, sort of—she talks to the bear more than me... (*She
winces and dries up*)

He stares a question

Never mind, explain later, it's the HRT—I get a surge about this time of
night...
Lazenby And you have a part-time job?
Norma Booth's Greeting Cards. No occasion too tacky. Packing and
Despatch. Three mornings a week. I know the verses by heart: "It's
impossible to thank you—for all the things you've done—to make a home
that's filled with love, and warmth, and jolly fun. And Mum, it's impossible
to find the words to say—how very dearly you are loved—today and *every
day*"!
Lazenby (*laughing*) You don't write them, I hope!
Norma (*gravely*) Oh no, Mr Heaney does that. We send a batch off quarterly:
"There you go, Seamus lad—stick some verses on 'em"!

*He laughs and she waits, smiling, until he stops. He sees her staring at her
empty glass and picks it up and stands*

Lazenby Refill? Of?
Norma Vodka and lime in a fresh glass, please.

He regards her

Lazenby I'm surprised a woman of your calibre needs to use a dating agency.
Norma (*sharply*) What calibre's that, then—twelve bore?
Lazenby Sorry, that was tactless...
Norma I'm not desperate, if that's what you think...
Lazenby Oh, obviously not! That's what I mean...

He stops and they let the awkward moment pass

How long does it take before you know it's time to "make your excuses and
leave" as the *News of the Screws* reporters have it?
Norma (*shrugging*) Ten, fifteen minutes usually—you?
Lazenby About the same.

They smile at each other

Pause

Hope you'll be here when I get back, *Norma*.

Lazenby goes off L

Norma checks her watch

Norma (*after a pause; murmuring*) Geoff Lazenby. There you go, then...

Black-out

A recording of Peggy Lee singing Sing a Rainbow *plays. In a spotlight, Lop Wink cycles on madly towards some unthinkable destination*

SCENE 5

Phoebe's room. The following morning

Phoebe is huddled on a chair by the bed, cuddling the bear and looking angry. She looks across to the open door

Phoebe (*shouting*) Norma! Where have you gone?

Pause

Norma!

Norma is offstage in the front room

Norma (*off; calling*) I'm coming! Keep your hair on!
Phoebe You've got me out of bed and just gone walkabout again! What are you doing?

Norma emerges from the front room with a Hoover and heads for the sitting-room

It's worse than being in hospital here! I'm like a fish out of water!
Norma (*pleasantly*) More like an old crab prised out of its shell... (*She enters the room, puts the Hoover down, starts to brush the bed sheets with a hand*)
Phoebe You went straight to bed last night without giving me a thought.

Norma hums Mr Wonderful *as she brushes the bed*

Were you tight?

Norma As a tick. Didn't you hear me singing?

Phoebe (*unsure*) You weren't...

Norma Four sheets to the wind, Mummy dear, rat-arsed, knickers on head, yodelling—the full dissipation.

Phoebe You could have stuck your head around the door just to see if I was still alive.

Norma I did, and you were.

Phoebe How did you know?

Norma (*absently*) Crumbs... There's enough crumbs in this bed to reconstitute a French stick.

Phoebe I could have been dead! How did you know?

Norma Music coming from both ends—snoring and t' other thing. Don't know how Mr Wonderful sticks it at times...

Phoebe Rubbish!

Norma (*finishing the bed*) Phoebe Green and her invisible trombone.

Phoebe I'd like to have seen you drunk—you've never let yourself go. Even as a girl you were nipped.

Norma hums again, pretending not to hear

Even as a baby. You came out of me looking as if you expected the worst.

Norma hums on as she plugs in the Hoover

And you took some getting out... Agony... Hours of it—I thought I'd never go to the toilet again.

Humming Mr Wonderful *even louder, Norma smiles at Phoebe as she gestures to open the bed*

Always a nipped-up little madam she was, Mr Wonderful—but of course you know—you were there. Even at her birthday parties she never let go.

Norma (*softly*) I left that to you.

Phoebe What?

Norma I was quiet, like Dad.

Phoebe Quiet? He was comatode—he let his own life pass him by—no go in him at all. I sometimes wonder how we got you.

Norma Back into bed then.

Phoebe He took some stirring.

Norma helps her mother back into bed. Cuddling the bear and groaning, she glares at Norma when re-installed

I hate it when you're like this.

Norma Like what?

Phoebe Happy.

Norma Thanks, Mummy.

Phoebe Nothing I say gets through to you when you're like this—you're impervient.

Norma (*going to the Hoover*) Impervious.

Phoebe And don't start with that thing, I can't stand it!

Norma picks up some old papers and heads for the door

I take it you had a good time, then?

Norma Better.

Phoebe How much better?

Norma Considerable improvement.

Phoebe You're not having me on?

Norma gives her a full smile and shakes her head

Victor Mature?

Norma Not exactly, but quite nice-looking. Been handsome once. Looks like a sad little boy at times. Divorced... (*She thinks of Lazenby, smiling*) A son down South somewhere, doesn't visit much, I got the impression... Has a Bentley Mark Six.

Phoebe A Bentley. Well...

Norma "Big Bore Saloon for a big bore" he said—but he *wasn't* boring.

Phoebe What was he?

Norma Teacher.

Phoebe (*impressed*) Oh... Have a decent pension then.

Norma laughs and heads for the door again

Mr Wonderful?

With her back to her, Norma shrugs, teasing

Possible?

Norma Probably not—not my type.

Phoebe What is your type, we ask ourselves—don't we, Mr Wonderful? (*She nods the bear's head from behind*) What's up with the poor man? No, don't tell me—he sniffs?

Norma shakes her head

He's got a twitch?

Norma shakes her head

Slurps? Trumps? Scratches his bits and pieces?
Norma (*laughing*) He looks like a bank manager.
Phoebe Oh well—write him off straight away!
Norma He's just so... He seems so well-adjusted... Nice... (*She shrugs*) I don't know about him.
Phoebe You'll never find your father, you know?

Norma gasps at this insight and goes to the dressing table as if to elude the thought. She stares into the mirror

Daddy's girl...
Norma Stop it.

Phoebe stops at the iron in Norma's voice

Pause

Phoebe Don't think you've got a type, anyway. It's been fifty-seven varieties with you—feasts and famines—out with every Tom, Dick and Harry— well, not Dick, I gather—then nothing for months. Sister Norma the sighing nun.

She watches Norma pick up police issue handcuffs

Norma Wonder what *Edward's* doing.
Phoebe Time probably—blasted prevert.
Norma Pervert.
Phoebe The Laughing Policeman—he was nuts.
Norma (*with a Welsh accent*) "How do you feel about letting me tie you up with Sellotape and brown paper, Norma", he said to me. I said: "I get enough of that at work". (*She puts the cuffs down and heads for the door*) I'll make some tea.
Phoebe What's his name?
Norma Geoff Lazenby.
Phoebe What happened last night?

Norma considers for a moment

Norma Let's just say—we exchanged something.
Phoebe Not these bodily fluids I keep hearing about, I hope?

Norma Something different happened. For the first time it was more than a set-up. I think. Something real happened. (*She looks elated for a moment, her smile on full beam, filling with hope*) I enjoyed myself. I went straight to bed to——
Phoebe Think about it.

Norma nods

(*Hit*) You'll be seeing him again, then.

Norma grins and goes out

I asked you a question, our Norma!

Norma goes along the passage, tripping and light as a teenager. Phoebe is distraught suddenly, cuddling the bear pitifully

Norma!

Norma has reached the foot of the stairs, where she stops and stares at herself in the mirror. She lowers her gaze to the phone below it

Norma He's going to ring me.
Phoebe What?
Norma He's got my number!
Phoebe Huh! We've heard that before! Another one bites the dust, eh, Mr Wonderful! He'll never ring…

Black-out

A recording of Peggy Lee singing It's All Right With Me *plays*

Lop Wink cycles in the background, hurtling nowhere in a strobe of moonlight, or across the stage in a semi-circle if possible

SCENE 6

The pub. About 9 pm, a fortnight later

Norma and Lazenby occupy the same chairs, with drinks etc. in front of them. She is listening

Lazenby Oh, it must be a marvellous job, but I can't make head nor tail of what he actually does. Don't understand all this computer jargon, do you?

Norma shakes her head

They make laptops or something—sounds like a breed of dog to me...

Norma smiles

Do you have a laptop, Norma?
Norma We've only just got the phone in.
Lazenby Anyway, he took the separation badly and blamed me, of course. Doesn't matter what age you split up, the kids don't want it to happen. We'd said for some time... (*He stops, shrugs, pained*) Oh, never mind, this must be boring for you.
Norma (*shaking her head*) What was wrong?
Lazenby Oh, any number of things, but really—the ravages of time. The depredations of use.
Norma I love it when you talk dirty.

He laughs. She smiles. They are relaxed together

Lazenby We'd simply worn each other out. It's an awful feeling when you look at this person you've invested your life in and... You want to scream: "please don't do that like that again. Please don't say that in that particular way—don't turn to me with that coquettish look I once found delightful but which now irritates me beyond belief." Do you know what I mean?
Norma Oh yeah.
Lazenby Needless to say we hadn't slept together for years before we...

Her expression stops him

Pause

Norma Didn't have to tell me that—that's your business.
Lazenby I wanted you to know.
Norma Yeah?
Lazenby I want things to be honest between us, Norma.
Norma There you go, then.
Lazenby This is it.

She laughs joyously

What's funny?

Norma This is it! I've said that for years!
Lazenby This is it?
Norma *This is it!*

They try a few more inflections, laughing

I want it on my gravestone: "This is it"…

Pause. They sober up

If I ever get married, I want it engraving inside my ring.
Lazenby This is it. (*He puts a hand on hers for the first time*)

She stares blankly at it

Norma I don't think I've got any mannerisms, but if I have I want you to tell me. Don't suffer in silence. Don't pretend…

He watches as she puts a hand to her mouth and fills with something very dark, heavy, emotional

Lazenby What is it, Norma?
Norma (*nodding, hit*) Get a life.
Lazenby What?
Norma That's what made me try the dating agency in the end—Mother had been going on at me and reading them out for ages but I'd never have dreamt of actually doing it. One day the nurse came to give her an MOT— pretty young thing, glossy—born-again Doris Day type—anyway, I was helping her, mithering on about how nothing ever happened to me and I didn't know where the time had gone and suddenly she looked at me and said: "For God's sake get a life"… I was destroyed for days. I began to hear it on buses, at work—even saw it graffiti'd on a bridge on the way to work: get a life, get a life. I do think—something—tells you what you should be doing if you've got the nous to listen.
Lazenby That's really quite profound, Norma.
Norma Me profound? That's a laugh—I was in Remedial at school before it was invented.
Lazenby *Intimations of Mortality.* Do you like William Wordsworth?
Norma Could you bear to meet my mother? (*She giggles*)

He releases her hand

Let me rephrase that—would you care to meet my mother?
Lazenby Yes, I'd like that very much.

Norma Don't get too excited, she's not the Queen Mum—at least I hope she's not, I mean—God, I'm babbling again!

He smiles and waits patiently

She keeps asking to meet you, that's what I'm trying to say—I warn you, though—she can be a right pain in the arse, excuse my French?
Lazenby German actually.
Norma What?
Lazenby People tend to say "Excuse my French" after uttering vulgarities but most of ours are Germanic in origin—Anglo-Saxon.

Norma stares at him wide-eyed and he laughs

Oh, Lord, once a schoolteacher, eh? Sorry!
Norma That's all right.

Pause

Pompous git.

He laughs just a shade falsely

Pause

He picks up her hand and examines it

Don't, I hate my hands.
Lazenby There's nothing wrong with them.
Norma Look at the veins, I've got see-through skin—and they're so thin… Mother's hands are just the same.

She is uneasy as he pores over her hand

Dry skin an' all—I use buckets of hand lotion. Always washing up, you see, and doing the veg in the sink—I get funny ideas doing the veg. Sturdy young carrots, curvy courgettes—I make myself blush at times. Could be heading for a scandal, eh? "Norma Green in Vegetable Abuse Case"…

He still holds her hand

What's the fascination? Want me to cross your palm with silver?

She gasps slightly as he brings the hand up and kisses the back of it

Lazenby Does your mother like chocolates?
Norma Something like that. It's good of you to come, Geoff…

He kisses her hand again

Lazenby You're trembling, Norma.
Norma Wait till me teeth start chattering…
Lazenby Tell me exactly what you are seeing behind those beautiful eyes.

She stares at him, stunned by this intimacy

Tell me.

She shakes her head and tries to free her hand, but he tightens his grip

Come on, Norma. What are you thinking about?
Norma Rowntree's Fruit Gums.

He shakes his head and lets go of her hand. They both laugh

I'm mad, sorry—I'm not like other people—I make connections of my own, sorry—I'm just *mad*.

They are both very still for a moment, staring at each other, close but not touching, intensely aware

Black-out

Peggy Lee sings Fever

Lop Wink cycles

SCENE 7

Phoebe's room. The following Sunday around tea time

The room is tidier than usual

Phoebe is looking spruce, combing her hair and looking in a hand mirror, with a tray on her lap and the bear beside her. She warbles a verse from This Is My Lovely Day *from* Bless the Bride

Norma comes from the kitchen with tea-service and sandwiches etc. on a tray

Norma enters and puts the tray on the bedside table

Phoebe stops singing

Phoebe So how do I address his Highness—Geoffrey?
Norma That's his name, Mummy dear.
Phoebe You're so full of yourself I could spit. What do you call him, Cleverclogs?
Norma (*smiling at her*) No, Geoff.
Phoebe Geoff. (*Like the Queen Mum*) Geoff. Would you partake of a cucumber sandwich, *Geoff*?

Norma loses her smile and looks uneasy

Norma You will behave?
Phoebe Behave, Lizzie, what can you mean? I trust one knows how to conduct oneself in the presence of a *Geoff*?
Norma (*dismayed*) Why are you doing your Queen Mum routine? You haven't done her for ages.
Phoebe Oh, trot along, Lizzie, you're not Queen yet, you know!
Norma If you spoil this for me...
Phoebe (*regarding her imperiously*) Strange wayward gel you are, Margaret—and I had such hopes for you once.
Norma I'm *Norma*—not Elizabeth, not Margaret, not Anne—Norma!

Phoebe is suddenly back to herself, wickedly grinning

Phoebe Why are you yelling names at me? I know your name, silly mare— what's come over you?
Norma What's come over *me*?

The front doorbell trills

Phoebe (*regally*) Avon calling...

Norma stares a severe warning at her mother, pointing like Kitchener

Norma No, Mother! I'm warning you... (*She hurries out along the hallway. She fluffs her hair in front of the mirror and heads for the door*)

Phoebe fluffs her nicely combed hair into a mad bird's nest and lies back across the pillows like a corpse

Norma admits Lazenby, who is dressed in a smart blazer etc. and is bearing flowers and a box of liquorice allsorts

Hallo.
Lazenby Norma…

Norma closes the door. He looks around the hallway

Norma It's all right, should be a listed "Dump"—you don't have to say "nice
Anaglypta" or anything.
Lazenby You look nice.

*She smiles full beam. He gives her the flowers and they move to the foot of
the stairs*

Norma Geoff… My mother can be a bit—unusual.
Lazenby It's all right, Norma.
Norma It's stress, I think, she's not used to company and was always pretty
giddy anyway. I mean something comes over her at times——
Lazenby Mrs Hyde?
Norma No, the Queen Mum—I should have explained—she's always doted
on the Royals and their recent troubles have only made her worse, but she
does it to make me mad and——
Lazenby (*interrupting*) Norma… It's all right… I think I can cope with one
rather eccentric old lady.

Norma stares at him a moment

Norma You are wonderful.

*Lazenby follows into the sitting-room. Phoebe is horribly agape. Norma
leads him to the foot of the bed and clocks this*

Mother, this is Geoff—Mother!
Lazenby Good grief…

Phoebe sits up as if nothing had happened

Phoebe Ew, one must have dropped orff. (*She smiles dottily at them*) Yes,
Margaret—whom hev we here?
Norma Geoff Lazenby.
Phoebe (*extending a hand*) How kaind of you to drop in, Lazenby.

Lazenby takes her fingers briefly

Lazenby Delighted to meet you, Mrs Green.

Phoebe (*brightly*) Verdigris.

Lazenby looks at Norma

Norma Take no notice. Flashback. Family joke. (*She glares at Phoebe*) Which I am not going to explain.
Phoebe Perhaps you know what verdigris is, Lazenby? One is surrounded by dimwits here...
Lazenby Ehr, green rust—on metal usually.
Phoebe (*to the bear in her normal voice*) Well, she was right, Mr Wonderful—he's a right knowledge box, proper cleverdick.
Norma Mother...

Phoebe smiles coquettishly at Lazenby and proffers one of the bear's paws

Phoebe Shake paws with my Companion of Honour, Geoff—he won't bite you.

Lazenby moves to the bedside and obeys

Lazenby Mr Wonderful. What an honour. Heard so much about you.
Phoebe (*in gruff bear's voice*) All bad, I hope!

Lazenby laughs. Phoebe giggles. Norma looks less anxious. Lazenby sits on a chair beside her

Lazenby Might I call you Phoebe? It's a lovely old name.
Phoebe It's ancient! I hate Phoebe! It makes me think of things hanging in wardrobes! Smelling of mothballs!
Lazenby (*calmly*) Comes from the Greek "Phoebus" who was Apollo's daughter if my memory serves me. I'll look it up for you.

Phoebe stares, impressed, slowly rotates the bear's head ditto

Norma There you go, then, Mummy dear—you're the daughter of a Greek god.
Lazenby Sun God actually.
Norma She can be fiery.
Lazenby Also means: "The bright one".

Phoebe preens

Norma (*dryly*) There you go, then.

Phoebe (*again as Queen Mum*) And hes one seen you at Glamis, Geoff?
Lazenby I'm afraid I've never been to (*correct pronunciation*) Glahms, ma'am.
Phoebe Ew, yew mast come, come next weekend, come and shoot something. See to it, Margaret.
Lazenby Delighted. Thank you, ma'am.

Pause

Norma and Lazenby exchange slightly embarrassed smiles. Phoebe becomes herself as she spots sweets on Lazenby's lap

Phoebe What you got there, then?
Lazenby Oh, for you—Phoebe. (*He puts the box of sweets on the tray*)

Phoebe simpers with pleasure as she opens the box and breathes in deeply

Phoebe Ouh… That first divine smell of lickerarse… (*She smiles sideways at Lazenby*) Can one tempt you to a lickerarse sandwich, Geoff?
Lazenby Not just now, thank you, ma'am.

Phoebe puts a coconut wheel in her mouth

Phoebe (*as Queen Mum*) Mr Wonderful and I have a nasty suspicion, Geoff…
Lazenby Really, ma'am?
Phoebe We suspect… (*She stops and chews and puts another sweet in her mouth*)

Norma and Lazenby watch and wait

The manuthatcherers are putting more and more lickerarse logs in! They are exceeding the quota per packet!

Lazenby shakes his head and tuts

One cannot rely on anything any more. But if I find out for certain, I shall revoke their warrant! See how they like that!
Norma I'll make the tea. (*She touches Geoff's arm*) Won't be long, Geoff. (*She heads for the door*)
Phoebe One supposes you've come to ask for Margaret's hand?

Norma whips round and glares at Phoebe—who returns to herself and grins

Or will you take all of her?

Phoebe and Lazenby laugh

Norma shakes her head and hurries anxiously into the kitchen

Pause

(*Confidingly*) I've disembowelled her financially, of course. She's got nothing coming to her. This entire estate is to be sold, proceeds to our favourite charity, eh, Mr Wonderful?
Lazenby Very commendable, ma'am.
Phoebe "Rescue the Dancing Bears" in Turkey. (*She cuddles Mr Wonderful tenderly*) His idea, of course—after we watched this terrible film on that thing (*she nods to the TV*) about those poor dear creatures tortured into performing on the streets. These marvellous people saved a group of them and took them to this sanctuary—this peaceful valley where they turned them loose, didn't they, Mr Wonderful? (*She nods his head*) The bears just shuffled away from the trucks and sat amongst the flowers at first. Under the olive and walnut trees. Mr Wonderful and I had a little weep together because it seemed deliverance had come too late—they were damaged beyond all help. And then... Oh, it was so beautiful, Lazenby, so touching. The bears began to dance under the trees. But not the horrid forced shuffling to and fro of the streets... They did their own dances. (*She rocks from side to side with the bear in her arms*) The camera drew away and the credits rolled and the bears went on waltzing, waltzing in the evening light. (*She stops and covers the bear's ears with her hands*) He's going in the coffin with me. I couldn't leave him with anyone else.

Lazenby nods. The kettle whistles off

She's disturbed, you know?
Lazenby Disturbed—Norma?
Phoebe She could run up a shutter any time. It's like walking on eggshells in this place—temper? You've no idea.
Lazenby I can't believe it...
Phoebe Oh, she seems quite normal, Geoff, I know. Most of the time she manages to control it, but if she does turn her hog out—watch out! (*She pauses*) Has she told you about her previous?
Lazenby Previous what?
Phoebe Oh, heck, she hasn't then...
Lazenby I know she's never married.
Phoebe You must have asked yourself why, Geoff? I mean, she's not just out of the box, is she? Oh, you men are innocent.

Lazenby I don't know what you're trying to say.

Phoebe (*shaking her head*) I blame these feminininists. Putting all this liberation into heads too small for it.

Lazenby Please, why hasn't Norma been married?

Phoebe She likes variety, Geoff. Beneath that rather unusual fashion sense lies a modern woman of the worst kind.

Lazenby shakes his head in confusion

She will not be tied, Geoff. She will not do anything she doesn't feel like doing one hundred per cent. She's a right little madam to be blunt.

Norma comes out of the kitchen and along the passage carefully with a teapot

I'm not saying she's a nympho, don't get me wrong, but that couch through there has had some hammer.

Lazenby What?

Phoebe Ouh, have I shocked you, Geoff? I just don't want you to blindly go where so many have gone before. I mean… (*She smiles coyly*) You're a cut above…

Norma enters

Phoebe goes on smiling at Geoff, and instantly reverts to Queen Mum mode

Would you like me to sing for you, Geoff?

Lazenby Ma'am, what a treat.

As she puts the teapot on the tray, Norma shakes her head at Lazenby frantically, but it's too late—Phoebe clears her throat and starts to warble Little Things Mean a Lot

Norma folds her arms resignedly

The Lights go down, denoting the passing of time

In the moment of darkness, Lop Wink gives an unmoving burst of energy— a spotlit transport of delight, or crosses the stage

When the Lights come up again, Lazenby and Norma are leaving the sitting-room. They stop in the middle of the hallway

Norma She'll sleep for ages now, I expect.

Lazenby Not surprised! We've been through the song book!
Norma *Every Song You've Ever Hated* by Phoebe Green. Talk about
humiliation.
Lazenby It wasn't that bad...
Norma We could sit in the front room... (*She indicates the doorway and a
glimpse of the couch*)

To her dismay, he checks his watch

Lazenby Love to, but I have things to do...
Norma Geoff...
Lazenby Yes, Margaret—sorry, Norma?

*She puts her arms about him and kisses him full on the lips. It's a badly timed
bodged attempt to restore the situation, which he gently tolerates, disengages
himself, and heads for the door*

(*Murmuring*) Afraid I must be on my way... (*He opens the door*) Good
night, Norma.

Lazenby goes out

Norma drifts numbly back to the hall mirror and regards her reflection

Norma Well... There you go, then. Good job I didn't try tongues. Oh, he
really loved that. That was cool, Norma, classy. (*She is suddenly furious,
frustrated, glaring*) Look at you! Great stupid mad cow! Lump! After all
this time! (*She pauses*) What came over you...?

Phoebe's voice comes drowsily through

Phoebe Has Mastermind gone, Norma? I could do with another cup of tea—
me throat's a like a donkey jacket sleeve.

Norma starts towards the stairs

Norma, love?

*Norma storms along the passage, making a growling sound in her throat and
crashes into the room and up to the foot of the bed. Phoebe smiles at her*

Didn't it go well...? I think he was quite impressed under his stuffed
shirt——

Norma It was a disaster, Mother! It was the full raging catastrophe and you
   know it!

Phoebe What are you on about?

Norma Don't pretend you don't know. The Queen Mum was out in all her
   glory—months and months you've let her rest, but tonight—tonight of all
   nights because you had something nasty to do, you woke her up... Well,
   you've done your dirty work all right—he's gone! It'll be a miracle if he
   comes back.

Phoebe Oh, go and make some Horlicks.

Norma I liked him. I really liked him! (*She realizes it herself and feels the
   first loss*) Why do you have to ruin things for me? Done it all my life one
   way or another.

Phoebe Don't talk so daft.

Norma It's true! Why did you get me into this dating crap? Just so you could
   do this?

Phoebe I didn't like him, Norma—too smooth, too calculating—he's dead
   at the back of his eyes, love.

Norma Since when have you been a judge of character? Or of anything?

Pause

   I didn't want to be hurt like this. I was doing all right on my own.

Phoebe You were turning into a cabbage, my girl! Mithering on day and
   night about nothing! I wanted you to join the human race!

Norma That's good coming from you! Do you realize how long you've
   spent in bed with that bloody animal? Bear-Pit Woman strikes again!

Phoebe Oh, dear Mr Wonderful, don't listen—there's a mad woman in the
   room.

Norma groans and heads for the door

   You've been a terrible daughter to me—nothing but a disappointment.

*Norma freezes between the bed and the door. She is bowed with pain and fury
for a moment, winded, then she comes up for air and turns*

Norma (*icily*) What did you say, *Mother*?

Phoebe You heard, you've been the death of me—you've made a cul-de-sac
   of me. Tate and Lyle. Unopened box. Untouched by human hand—that's
   you!

Norma stands at the foot of the bed, shaking her head

   You could have given me a grandchild!

Norma Don't you... Don't you dare... You're a child yourself, always have been.

Phoebe Nonsense.

Norma Dad brought us up, not you—whenever I needed you, you were off with the fairies—or some bloke!

Phoebe Stop, stop, Norma, I'm not well...

Norma moves closer beside the bed

Norma (*shouting*) You were the goer of this family, Mother! And you wonder why I've had difficulties with men—I hate it when they come on to me—I want it but I hate it. You've damaged me, don't you see? I don't really believe anyone could love me—I can't *give* because there doesn't seem to be much there. *I'm all front.*

Phoebe (*hit*) Oh, go to bed, Margaret, you've had too much gin.

Norma There you go, running away—don't give me that crap about grandchildren—you never liked kids. Play with me, Mummy? Play with me? Kids bored you to death—*I* bored you! Shy at my parties, was I? I was embarrassed because you were there being sarcastic or acting the giddy goat while poor old Dad tried to hold it together. You were drunk once, Mother—singing and tossing jelly about! (*She stops, thinks*) What did you say to Geoff?

Phoebe Just a few home truths.

Norma Like what?

Phoebe Just a few fibs.

Norma Oh God.

Phoebe I'm sorry...

Norma (*shaking her head*) This time, I thought it might be different, this man, I thought—this man might love me as I need to be loved. He might really be tender and caring and bring me out of myself.

Phoebe I'm sorry, Norma—really I am. (*She starts to snuffle, clutching Mr Wonderful to her bosom and dabbing her face with a tissue*)

Norma I was beginning to really like him. (*She turns to her mother*) How could you hurt me like this?

Phoebe wails and suddenly Norma is holding her

Phoebe I could see that! I could see you'd clicked at last. I don't want to be left on my own!

Shocked and staring, Norma moves on to the bed until she is sitting behind Phoebe and the old lady rests in her arms like a frail child. Phoebe snuffles and snuggles against her body

(*Mumbling*) Say you won't leave me, Norma, say you won't put me in a home. You're all I've got. I'm your *mother.*

Norma looks down at her, still angry, but unable to speak

Don't leave me, there's a good girl. What would I do? Norma…

Norma stares down at Phoebe's face as her eyes close and the Light slowly closes in. Just before darkness gulps them down, Norma stares straight ahead as if numbed by the reality of her situation

Norma (*murmuring*) Mother.

Black-out

ACT II

SCENE 1

The pub. A fortnight later

Love is Strange by Buddy Holly is swirling faintly on the jukebox in the background

Norma is sitting in her usual chair, with an empty glass and folded newspaper in front of her, looking bored, impatient. She looks around, sighs, picks up the paper

Norma (*reading; dryly*) "Lop Wink. Unusual name for unusual gent. International person. Wealthy, super-fit. Ex jet-setter returned to roots for new beginning with suitable, 'sexy' in brackets, lady". Well, I guess your landing was delayed. A Lop's as good as a wink to me.

She looks R and sees Lop Wink, in biking gear, trotting in: rhubarb and custard-coloured lycra, bulging crotch, cycling helmet, gloves, etc. up to the table

Oh, my godfathers.
Wink Norma Green?
Norma Lop Wink.

He bounces into the chair beside her and grins. She smiles back wanly. He removes his helmet from his sweat-plastered head

Wink (*with a rapid delivery*) What you got to say for yourself, then? Don't tell me—where'd you get a name like that? Dutch extraction of course, spent years working around the Amsterdam area, but love England really, too flat over there, as Noël Coward so perceptively remarked—great biking country, but not challenging enough for a guy like me. What were you going to say, Norma? Was I right?
Norma I was going to say: come on a bit from a pair of cycle clips and a scarf round the gob, haven't we?
Wink Thought I'd bike here, hope you don't mind. Bike everywhere now

I'm a gentleman of leisure, got six bikes in the garage—no car, don't need one, don't believe in 'em, got to stop all this pollution. Be driving round in a desert if we don't—don't you agree, Norma? Weather's gone haywire as it is—don't you agree, Norma? You get much exercise, Norma?

Norma (*stunned by his machine-gun delivery*) Oh, y'know, occasional twenty mile road bash before breakfast.

Wink Kidding me, of course, still, I can take it. There's no buzz like the natural buzz of a super-fit mind in a super-fit body, Norma, let me assure you of that. (*He jumps up, runs on the spot then sits again*)

Norma There you go then, Lop.

He flexes an arm before her

Wink Feel that, Norma.

Norma Do I have to…?

Wink Go on, feel it.

She does so gingerly

Is that the bicep of a forty-five-year-old man?

Norma You're going to tell me.

Wink Rhetorical question, Norma—course it isn't. Well, I am forty-five and I can see you're amazed—but there are men of thirty who couldn't hold a bicep up to mine *and* Shazam!

He springs to his feet and batters both fists on his tensed abdomen, much to Norma's horror

That's what I call a six-pack, Norma! Hard as bell metal! Want to punch it? (*He swivels himself towards her*)

Norma stares straight ahead

And as for these—pistons! Iron hard! Thunder Thighs they call me at the club! (*He pummels his outer legs and thighs*) Years of pounding the roads gone into them! Mountains of Mourne, Scottish Highlands, Trossachs, Snowdonia. What do you say, Norma?

Norma (*softly but fiercely*) Sit down!

Wink I beg your pardon!

Norma Sit down, you great kid! What do I care about your body? You come in here like a damn great stick of rhubarb and start making an exhibition of yourself! *Sit down*!

Shattered, Wink subsides into his chair

Pause

What's the matter with you?

Wink Sorry, Norma. I was determined to make an impression this time. Had
so many knock-backs when I come as meself I thought...

Norma You'd come as an alien who got off his spaceship and found a bike?

Wink Well! Who knows what you women want? Buggered if I do.

Norma Honesty's not a bad start—being yourself. It's nice to *talk*.

Wink I'm not really from Amsterdam.

Norma Go on—I was convinced you were a retired diamond merchant.

Wink looks totally demoralised

Where did you work?

Wink Co-Op. (*He pauses*) Drove that bloody butcher's van for thirty years.

Norma Where did you get the name—*Star Trek*?

Wink Name's real—my dad came from Utrecht.

Norma There you go, then.

Wink I did go, that's what broke me heart, Norma.

Norma What d'you mean?

Wink Coupla year ago I went on a fortnight's holiday to Utrecht. Hired a
bicycle and just rode about. For the first time since I were a kid I felt happy.
Free.

Norma I haven't had a holiday for years.

Wink Don't, holidays can damage your health.

Norma So you met a Dutch girl and she broke your heart?

Wink (*shaking his head*) Not she—it—the place. Thinking of another life
I might have lived instead of riding about with a load of rotting flesh for
decades! I knew I'd wasted my life, Norma.

Norma (*touched*) This is it.

Wink You know what I mean?

Norma nods gravely

That's why I ride, Norma, I live on my own, y'see, since the court case and
I just *ride*. Started out as an 'obby, but now it's something else. I have to
exhaust meself so I can't feel anything, Norma—it's like I'm trying to get
somewhere. I know I'll never get there but I've got to keep trying. It's a
kind of praying motion, Norma, can you understand that? It's like a kind
of sacrifice.

She stands and he gazes up at her

You're not going, Norma... Why are you going now we've got talking,
Norma? You said you liked to talk...

Norma Sorry, Lop, you've lost me.

He holds her arm, keeping her beside him

Wink You think I'm boring, don't you, Norma—you think I'm Joe Soap
from Rochdale, but I don't just ride ordinary, Norma—sometimes I ride
unusual—sometimes I ride at night down country lanes with... (*He
glances around then whispers something into her ear*)

*Norma's expression goes cool, cold, arctic, minus zero. She stares straight
ahead as the Lights go down slowly, unblinking but blanking Wink as he
pours something very personal into her fastidious mind*

Black-out

Peggy Lee sings It Never Entered My Mind

SCENE 2

Phoebe's room. About an hour later

*Phoebe is sitting in bed with the bear beside her—watching flickering TV,
knitting, chewing allsorts*

*Waves of tinny mirth come from the set, but her glum expression doesn't
waver*

Norma enters and locks the front door behind her

*She glances at herself wearily in the mirror, then enters the sitting-room and
switches the TV off*

Phoebe I was watching that.

Norma It's time you were asleep.

Phoebe Still crabby, are we? She's crabby, Mr Wonderful—she went out
crabby and she's come back crabby—she's been crabby for a fortnight,
hasn't she? Crabby as her bottom.

Norma Do you want a drink?

Phoebe (*as Royalty*) Noew, thenk you—we've had an elephant sufficiency
of beverages this evening. You can put the corgis out and...

She stops at Norma's look

Norma No more Queen Mum—I've told you—there'll be a sudden liquorice allsorts shortage!

Phoebe sulks, cuddling the bear. Norma sighs

   Any phone calls?
Phoebe Just one.

Norma stares a burning question: who?

   (*To the bear*) A Mr V. Mature called, didn't he? (*She nods the bear from behind*) Requesting a date with *moi*.
Norma Oh, yeah, ten thirty at the boneyard—bring your own skin?
Phoebe (*to the bear*) Ouh, she can be so nasty, can't she? Don't know where she gets it from.

Pause

Norma turns towards the door

Norma I'm going to bed.
Phoebe What was he like—Wop Link?
Norma Lop Wink.
Phoebe Did he have ears like Mr Spock?
Norma He was sad. Another Rochdale Cowboy.
Phoebe I like Americans.
Norma We know, Mummy dear.
Phoebe They have real men's voices. Victor Mature had a voice that gave you goose-pimples.
Norma I can't saddle myself with the Lop Winks of this world! I can't help being normal and wanting normal things! It's getting abnormal to be bloomin' normal these days!
Phoebe I take it you didn't click, then.
Norma With a mad cyclist? More gears on his bike than brain cells? On the Social and still wanting to ride around the back lanes of a night wi' nowt on but talcum powder?
Phoebe What do you mean?
Norma I've been out with another sicko, Mother! God knows what happens if he gets a puncture—oh, I've had enough. (*She stands by the door, shaking her head*) I dunno what's happened to men. Why can't they be like they used to be in old films? John Mills wouldn't dream of riding a

mountain bike bare buff! Tyrone Power didn't have a fixation about
screws—not the metal sort, anyway.
Phoebe Victor Mature was a real man. Lovely dark eyes he had, dark as...
Norma Tarmac on a wet night on the M62.
Phoebe Liquorice logs in little bowls of milk.

*They look at each other and laugh gently. Norma moves to the bedside and
sits, regarding her mother*

Norma I'm giving up this dating lark.
Phoebe I still don't believe what they said about Rock Hudson. Lovely big
man like that—I'll never believe it. What?
Norma I'm giving it up—no more dates with Desperate Dans for me.
Phoebe You've wasted some money.
Norma (*shrugging*) I'm a bit wiser for it.
Phoebe And older.

Norma smiles at her, forcedly

Pause

Geoffrey was *nice*.
Norma Nice? Compared with the others he was Mr Darcy in his blouse. (*She
sighs*) I can't do it any more. Every time I come back from a date, that
mirror takes a slice off me—it's a hope-slicer.
Phoebe Oh, stop mithering.
Norma I'm finished with all that. If Mr Wonderful doesn't come along
naturally I shall do without.

The front doorbell trills

Phoebe Who's that this time of night? Don't answer it.
Norma Don't be so daft. (*She hurries out to the front door*)
Phoebe Keep the chain on! No strangers!

Norma passes the mirror with a glance and a groan and opens the door

Lazenby is there

Norma Hallo, stranger.
Phoebe (*yelping*) Norma!
Lazenby Can I come in?

*Norma stands aside and he enters, sheepish, with a monster box of liquorice
allsorts*

Phoebe Who is it?
Norma Geoff! We're going in the front room! (*She shows him into the front room*)

Phoebe looks miffed and jealous

Phoebe (*shouting*) No monkey business!
Norma (*wryly*) Monkey business... I'm nearly fifty.

Pause

Sit if you like, it's...
Lazenby Same price as standing, I know.

They sit on the couch, well apart. He puts the sweets down between them

Norma Three pound box? She'll change her will for you—sod the dancing bears.

Pause

In the sitting-room, Phoebe strains sideways out of the bed towards the door, listening

Lazenby Norma, I'm sorry.
Norma Your life's your own, Geoff.
Lazenby I just... One gets cautious... Things suddenly seemed to be moving rather fast.
Norma You'd met 'er through there—the Mad Mullah—it'd give anyone pause for thought. But she is part of the package—I'd never farm her out.
Lazenby It's the commitment I find hard...
Norma Join the club.
Lazenby I keep saying to myself I'm lonely, I'm sad—I want a steady relationship again, but when I come face to face with it—it's frightening.
Norma This is it, tell me about it.

They stare at each other

Lazenby I have missed you.

She nods

Pause

Norma What did the Mad Mullah say to you?

Lazenby (*shaking his head*) I don't want to cause trouble...

Norma You can't, there isn't a trouble we haven't had, but we go on. Tell me?

Lazenby I didn't believe her for a moment...

Norma stares at him: what?

Well, she hinted that you were a woman of easy virtue, shall we say.

Norma laughs and looks at the door

Norma You rotten old bat!

Pause

Nothing could be more untrue about me. She was the goer of the family—God, she was like a traffic light stuck on green: Yanks, blokes down the pub, just about drove my father demented. I'm what she calls me now and then: "Tate and Lyle—untouched by human hand". Well, touched here and there but not deeply. Not deeply enough.

Lazenby (*interested*) My God, that is unusual these days.

Norma Oh, I know we're all supposed to have been at it hammer and tongs since we got out of nappies, but for one reason or another—*I* haven't.

Lazenby I'm—impressed.

Norma Sheer panic sometimes. Just had to get off the bus before the terminus.

Pause

Though I've longed to get there.

Pause

Teacher?

Lazenby Can we start again, Norma?

Norma Thought you were frightened?

Lazenby Yes, but more frightened of turning into a fusty old singleton. I think it's admirable that you've... Waited so long.

Norma Sorry I pounced on you like that.

Lazenby Don't mention it—normally I'd have been delighted.

Norma Normally. What a lovely word that is.

Lazenby Well, it contains your name.

She moves closer to the allsorts box. He turns towards her more. Phoebe
leans farther out of the bed on the far side, straining towards the door

Norma Kissed my first boyfriend on this couch: Michael Dobson. Our love
had blossomed when we discovered we both had psoriasis. Mother came
in just as we were getting down to business and screamed at him to get out.
Then she smacked my legs. "How far have you gone with him? Have you
gone all the way, you mucky little madam?" God, my legs stung. I cried
for hours in bed. (*She smiles sweetly and sadly*) Talk about humiliation.
Lazenby She shouldn't have done that.
Norma (*grinning*) Don't worry, hasn't made me like spanking or owt like
that—I'm an old-fashioned girl.
Lazenby Glad to hear it.

Pause

They are almost touching now. All senses switched full on

Norma Can you remember your first kiss?
Lazenby Phew! Now you're asking, not sure that I can…
Norma Oh, surely…

In the room, Phoebe is all rump as she strains towards the door. Lazenby
thinks hard

Lazenby There was a chubby girl with long blonde hair. Bit older than
myself. In a garden somewhere.
Norma Sounds promising.
Lazenby Very blonde, almost platinum—blowing bubbles with a clay pipe.
Soap and water in a bowl. She bossed me around terribly, poked and teased
and laughed at me. Then she tied me to this apple tree and kissed me with
her stinging soapy lips.

Norma chuckles, puts the allsorts box on the floor, smiles

Amazing how things come back. I was really quite scared of her,
humiliated like you. Wanted my mummy. I'm sure I cried, I thought she'd
never untie me.
Norma Eeh, precocious little madam.
Lazenby Yes. Never liked being tied up since—in any sense—I was married
a long time, but can't say I *liked* it—always felt the ropes chafing. Always
felt *tied*.
Norma There you go, then.

They stare, very close

Lazenby This is it.
Norma Oh, muck or bloody nettles—come here! (*She grabs him and kisses him on the mouth*)

This time he responds and things are hotting up, the couch creaking loudly. Then suddenly he draws back

What is it? Don't you want this?
Lazenby God, yes, but not here—listen, Norma, I know this little hotel in Southport...
Norma Oh, bugger Southport, Geoff! (*She starts kissing him again*)

Again he responds and in the sitting-room Phoebe goes out of view of the audience with a yell and a loud thump to the floor

Phoebe Norma! I've fallen out of bed!

They stop, breathing heavily. Norma glares at the wall

Lazenby She could be hurt, broken bones...
Norma I hope it's her neck.

Phoebe starts to wail like an air-raid siren. Norma gets up and goes calmly into the hallway and Lazenby follows

Shurrup, Mother, I'm coming!

At the foot of the stairs Norma trails a finger down the side of Lazenby's face to his chin, then goes towards the door. He watches her go

Phoebe I can't move! I can't move my legs or anything! Something went crack in my side, Norma!

Lazenby starts to follow Norma

Norma!

Black-out

Peggy Lee sings Somebody Loves Me

SCENE 3

Phoebe's room. Two weeks later. Mid afternoon

An expensive suitcase stands in the hallway

In the sitting-room, dressed for a trip away, Lazenby is laughing and teasing Phoebe with a bottle of Tia Maria, snatching it away as she grabs for it

Phoebe Oh, oh! You bad man! Oh, don't make me laugh any more, Geoff— my ribs are killing me!

He lets her have the bottle and she winks and buries it under her mound of pillows

So kaind...
Lazenby Fancy you knowing the one about the ten-inch pianist! I heard it in the Navy! I'm beginning to think you're a woman with a past, Phoebe Green...
Phoebe Oh, I am, I've had my moments!

Something buzzes and Lazenby takes a flash new mobile phone from a pocket and checks the screen

What you got there, then?
Lazenby (*switching it off*) Just a little gizmo my son sent me—haven't quite got the hang of it yet.
Phoebe Is that a gizmo in your pocket or have you taken a liking to me?

They both laugh. She holds out a hand

Can I hold it, Geoff?

With slight reluctance he hands it over

Lazenby Amazing instrument, I gather—seven functions, memory, recall— Lord knows what else—it can store a stack of callers.

Phoebe coos fascination and they lean over the mobile on her lap. He murmurs something indistinctly and they both laugh

Norma hears this as she comes into the hallway with a cheaper, smaller suitcase. She puts the case down outside Phoebe's door and enters

Hallo. Your mother's been giving me the story of her life.

Norma Doesn't ten minutes pass slowly sometimes…

Phoebe It's been a sight more interesting than yours, madam. (*She squeezes Lazenby's arm and winks at him*) He's brought me his gizmo, haven't you, Geoff? (*She holds up the mobile phone*) I've been playing with it—got more functions than your father ever had!

Norma (*to Lazenby*) I thought you hated things like that.

Lazenby I do, I did…

Phoebe Can I keep it, Geoff? To ring you if anything goes wrong?

Lazenby looks reluctant again

Norma You've got our telephone, Mother.

Phoebe I want his gizmo! Please, Geoff? I'm a bit worried about being left all on my own.

Lazenby (*shrugging, but worried; to Norma*) I don't want to leave it here…

Norma Oh, go on, you'll get it back tomorrow.

Phoebe Oh, thank you! Look, Mr Wonderful—a new toy. (*She shows the mobile phone to the bear and fiddles with it proudly*)

Lazenby pecks Norma's cheek and regards her

Lazenby You look terrific—all set?

Norma nods, somewhat nervous

Phoebe How about a kiss for me? (*She puckers up at Lazenby*)
Lazenby How can I resist?

He kisses Phoebe and shakes Mr Wonderful's paw when she proffers it

Be good, you two.

Phoebe It's me what should be saying that!

Norma Sure you'll be all right, Mummy dear?

Phoebe Course I will, it's only one night really. We'll be glad of a bit of peace and quiet, won't we, Mr Wonderful?

The bear nods with her help

Norma We can be back in forty minutes if you need us.

Phoebe Get away with you! And remember, Geoff… (*Coyly*) If a thing's worth doing, it's worth doing twice!

Norma sighs

Norma (*to Lazenby*) My case is outside, love.

Lazenby exits and takes her case to the front door where he waits, jiggling coins and keys in his trouser pocket and looking with some approval at himself in the mirror

Norma kisses her mother and the bear

You've got your painkillers and everything? Plenty of tissues, allsorts...
Phoebe Yes yes! What time's Mrs Thing from next door coming to check I'm still alive?
Norma Mrs Costayannis will look in first thing in the morning—be nice to her? It's not her fault they still have performing bears in remote parts of Turkey.
Phoebe What's the hotel called?
Norma *The Sea Brink*! It's all written on your pad.
Phoebe (*blankly*) Have a lovely time.

Norma stands staring until Phoebe looks up

Norma I'm a bit nervous.
Phoebe Oh, it'll come to you once you get going.
Norma Not about that! Well, a bit about that—but the whole thing really.
Phoebe He's a bit of all right, our Norma—he's a gentleman. I wish you'd met him years ago.
Norma So do I... (*She looks down at her breasts*) When these were more like chapel hat pegs than sandbags...
Phoebe Oh, come here, daft-head.

Norma goes to the bedside and her mother embraces her. They kiss again, holding hands

Love knows everything, love sees all and forgives all—love is kind. (*She regards Norma, still holding one hand*) My daughter's good enough for any man.

Norma is hit, staring as Phoebe releases her hand

Norma You've got the remote for the telly?
Phoebe Have I ever not? Go on, girl! Give him one for me.

Norma laughs ruefully and shakes her head. Somewhat choked with emotion, she exits and goes out to the waiting Lazenby. He gives her a boyish grin and she grins back then sobers and looks back at the door

Norma Isn't it funny. I've been looking forward to this for days—but I can
hardly bear to leave her now.
Lazenby You'll be fine ten miles down the road.
Norma In your stylish old banger! I'm so excited.
Lazenby Come on.

Lazenby goes out with the cases, leaving the front door ajar

Norma looks at herself in the mirror

Norma There you go, then, Norma Green. This is it—terminus.

Norma laughs and goes out, trailing a shout

Bye, Mother!

*She closes the door and turns the key in the lock. Phoebe is stilled in the bed
as she listens for the sound of the car starting and leaving, which it does*

*The Light turns golden and tarnishes and darkens and starts to close in
around the figure on the bed. Phoebe is suddenly just an old, vulnerable,
isolated woman cuddling a ragged teddy bear*

Her expression says all this a moment before Black-out

A recording of Andy Williams singing Days of Wine and Roses *plays*

SCENE 4

Phoebe's room. Later the same night

*Phoebe is sitting beside Mr Wonderful with a glass of Tia Maria in one hand,
the bottle on the table nearby. The mobile phone lies on the bed close to her
shrouded legs*

TV flickers mutely

Slightly tipsy, Phoebe croons a verse from You Belong To Me *(Anne Shelton)*

*The song dies out and she looks awfully bored, nostalgic and sorry for herself.
She stops and speaks to the bear*

Phoebe They've left us, Mr Wonderful, dear old boy. They've gone off to consume the relationship and left us to our own advices. In the end does anybody care about a silly old woman and her bear? Do they knickers. Once S-E-X rears its lovely head, that's it—job's over—the nice ties are slung overboard... Well! I've still got Tia Maria—my good fairy! (*She toasts the air*) Jolly good luck to them, say I! Shappy hagging! Yerss indeed... (*She drinks and falls silent, brooding*)

The mobile bleeps as a message is stored. She stares at it

That blurry thing's got a life of its own. Bleeping and carrying on. (*She giggles*) At least I can say I've slept with Geoff's gizmo, Mister Wunnerful, eh? (*She picks the mobile up and focuses on its display with some difficulty. She reads aloud*) Sea Drink Hotel... (*She giggles*) Sea Brink, you old wazzock. She'll be enjoying herself. She'll be all right. Making up for lost time... (*She presses a few buttons at random on the mobile*)

Nothing happens and she reads from the display again

Memory. Voice mailbox... Call...

She presses a series of numbers and jumps a bit at the sound of the operator's tape

Operator (*on tape*) Thank you for calling Couples Connect on your voice mailbox number. The following messages have been stored...

Several women's voices follow, husky, strident, common, posh, of a certain age

Woman 1 (*on tape*) Geoff, what happened at the weekend? What went wrong? We were expecting you—waiting for you. Chelsea was so upset— I know you didn't promise to come to the party, darling, but... Please get in touch? I love you, the kids love you—Geoffrey.

Phoebe listens, staring, amused at first. The voice-over on the sound system gets louder

Woman 2 (*on tape; distraught*) Geoffrey darling, why haven't you rung me back? I've left a dozen messages on this thing since Sunday—please please ring? You know how I feel about you... Surely we can just *talk*? I know you detest this emotional stuff, but I'm just about going out of my mind. (*She is breaking up*) Please, Geoffrey...?

Phoebe tuts and listens avidly now, gaping

Woman 3 (*on tape*) Hallo, cultured, scholarly gentleman, loved your ad. I'm
Mary Reed—a luscious mature blonde—even if I do say it myself… I do
aromatherapy and reflexology in a combined course of treatments from
my home or at your home should you so desire? (*With a throaty laugh*) My
business card reads: "Have Scents—will travel". Here's my number if
you'd like to give me a try? 01653 432169…

Pause

Woman 4 (*on tape*) Geoff, it's Sarah. God, last night was so good, my darling
man—you were almost too much for me. When can we do it again? I know
you're all over the place for a while and so am I dammit—but I just had to
say… (*She moans softly*) I'll be at the *Prince of Wales* Hotel number
tomorrow night. A filthy phone call would cheer me up no end…? Oh God,
great slobbery showery soapy shafting kisses to my fantastic man—my
dream lover…

*Phoebe holds the phone away from her face at the sounds of the woman
moaning in mock ecstasy, kissing the air, etc.*

Phoebe Mucky bitch.
Woman 4 (*on tape*) Geoff, you are a dream come true. *Wonderful*… Bye!

*Phoebe slowly lies back across the pillows as the full import of the voices
sinks in. She keeps the phone to her ear, and her changing expressions convey
shock, fascination, amazement, disgust*

Phoebe He *didn't*… I didn't know you *could*… Ouh… Preverts! (*She tuts
and shakes her head*)

*The Light closes in around her. She lifts the mobile up and shakes it, dismayed
and impotent*

Norma!

Black-out

Peggy Lee sings Small Hotel

SCENE 5

Sea Brink Hotel, *Southport. Next morning*

The sound of seagulls faintly in the background

*Norma is sitting at the table with cafetière, two cups, etc. on a tray before her.
She looks happy, reflective, relaxed—replete after a night of love*

After a moment, the Waiter approaches

Waiter Mrs Lazenby?
Norma No… (*She checks herself*) I mean yes—yes?
Waiter You had a phone call last night, timed at (*he looks at a slip of paper*)
one thirty-five a.m., and charged to your room number. (*He places the slip
on the table in front of her*) It would have been put through, but your
husband was adamant about not being disturbed.
Norma Who took this?
Waiter Night porter. Gone home. (*He stares a moment longer, then sits* R
at a small table, checking bills, etc.) Have a nice day, madam.
Norma (*drily*) Ta very much. (*She looks at the slip again and reads aloud*)
"Wolf! Wolf! Ring home Tia-Maria'd, but bear bears all below". (*She
glances at the phone on the wall and is about to get up*)

Lazenby breezes in from L, *in a white shirt, Royal Auto Club tie, linen
jacket,* Financial Times *under his arm*

Lazenby Hallo, you.
Norma (*fondly, shyly*) Hallo.

He leans over and kisses her cheek

Lazenby It's pretty bracing out there—nothing like a walk on the prom
before brekkie, eh! Ah, I see you've got some Java on the go… (*He sits
beside her and senses something's amiss*) You all right, my love? (*With an
accent*) My sexy *thang*…
Norma (*withholding the slip*) Mother left a message to phone her last
night—reads like ET's mother sent it.
Lazenby Well, touching base I suppose—missing you.
Norma I should have warned you about Tia Maria.
Lazenby How did you know? She asked me to smuggle it in…
Norma She had that Tia Maria twinkle in her eyes. I bet she was a right state
when she rang—it sends her bonkers.

Lazenby I'm sorry, Norma...
Norma (*shrugging*) I'd better ring her—she'll be feeling hellish—full of
alcoholic remorse.

He puts a hand on hers

Lazenby It'll keep while we have coffee together. (*He depresses the plunger
on the cafetière slowly, smiling*) Always feel there should be an explosion
nearby when I do this.
Norma The explosion was last night.

They smile at each other, intimately, happily

Lazenby What does man of woman desire? The lineaments of gratified
desire. What does woman of man require? The lineaments of gratified
desire.
Norma That's lovely.

Pause

She watches him pour coffee into the cups

Thank you for last night. For your tenderness.
Lazenby Thank *you*...
Norma I didn't know you could talk to someone for hours and still be
fascinated. I loved that deep sense of peace... Afterwards... (*She trails a
finger down the side of his face to his chin*) You've moved me. I feel like
a woman again. I know you said "Let's just take it a step at a time", but I'm
very close to falling over the brink.
Lazenby The Sea Brink?
Norma Into love with you, Geoff.
Lazenby We've got all the time in the world...
Norma Yes. Isn't it wonderful? I'm *happy*... Right now, right this minute—
this *is it*.
Lazenby (*stirred*) Let's go to our room.
Norma (*feeling his desire*) Eeh, they say it's quiet dog that takes a bite. Right
little raver, aren't you beneath that RAC tie?

They stand up together and are heading off R when the phone on the wall rings

The Waiter picks it up. They pass him and he calls after them

Waiter Miss Green? Is there a Miss Green?

Norma and Lazenby stop. He laughs at her expression

Lazenby Admit it—nobody gives a damn about that sort of thing these days.
Norma I'm Miss Green.
Waiter (*camp*) Ouh, hyphenated, are we...?

Lazenby drifts back to the table as she takes the phone from the smirking waiter and puts it to her ear. The waiter goes back to his table. Lazenby picks up a sugar cube, pops it into his mouth and crunches it placidly. He slowly realizes Norma is staring across the room at him. He grins and holds up another cube between first finger and thumb

Lazenby Tate and Lyle? For energy?

He sees that her animation has gone, she is slowly losing her radiance, her power—as some bad news sinks in. He goes to her as she replaces the receiver and faces him

Who?
Norma Mrs Costayannis.
Lazenby Oh, dear, not...?

Norma nods. Her face is bleak, blank, as she stands before him, struggling to absorb the news. A moment of stillness. Seagulls suddenly a shade louder and harsher outside. Lazenby takes her gently in his arms

Black-out

Peggy Lee sings He's a Tramp

SCENE 6

Norma's house. About an hour later

Mid-morning sunlight showing no mercy on dusty surfaces and the sitting-room still in disarray with Mr Wonderful sitting alone on the empty bed

A key turns in the lock and Norma enters with Lazenby behind, carrying cases

He puts the cases down. She turns, thinks

Norma So quiet... I feel as if I'd have known even if I hadn't just seen her at the Chapel of Rest—I'd have walked in and felt her ... absence.

He nods. She smiles gratefully at him

Thanks for taking me there.

He shakes his head, nobly

I'll be OK now.
Lazenby Are you sure? I mean, I'll help you do whatever has to be done.
Norma I'm not going to do anything today. I'm not going to touch anything yet…
Lazenby There will be things to see to, Norma. Death certificate—sorry, but… (*He stops and shrugs*) When my mother died it took days, it was unbelievably exhausting.
Norma I'll see to all that—but not today. (*She waits*)

He realizes she wants him to go

Lazenby Well, I'll leave you to your thoughts. You have my number if you need me.

She nods and smiles at him, loving him but wanting him gone for now. He backs towards the door

Anything at all. (*He reaches the door*) If you come across my mobile… (*He puts a crooked hand to his ear and mouth*) Son said I should start a New Luddite Party! I intend to show him. (*He looks as if he's ready to go*) Are you sure?
Norma I'm very tired, Geoff… (*She smiles*) Beautifully worn out, thanks to you. I just want to lie down. I want to think about her. (*She goes to him quickly and strokes his face*) It was lovely, lovely.

Lazenby goes out with a wry smile

Norma turns the key in the lock. She passes the mirror without a glance and enters the sitting-room. She walks to the end of the bed and stares at the tousled sheets, books, allsorts, the placid bear

You bare-faced bloody survivor… See us all out, you will.

Pause

She stands with her hands on the bed rail and thinks about her mother. She puts a hand over her tremulous lips as things come flooding back, coupled with the brutal fact

There you go then, Mother. This is it. Tried all my life to please you, but I was never quite the little princess you had in mind, was I...? Pity you couldn't hang on just a bit longer—all I wanted was to come back here and show you I was capable of happiness—that you hadn't damaged me beyond helping. (*She pauses*) Silly old slapper, why couldn't you be here? Just for once! (*She starts to break up after this angry shout*) Sorry, sorry... (*Unable to go on, she gets on to the bed and lies on her side in the trough of the bedclothes. Slowly she assumes the foetal position, with her face hidden by the bear. She lies like this for a moment, then pulls the bear down and cuddles it as she starts to sob: the mobile phone is revealed*)

Black-out

After a moment, Peggy Lee sings I'm a Woman

SCENE 7

Norma's house. A fortnight later

In Phoebe's room all is tidy, almost spartan, the bed stripped to ticking mattress and piled pillows. Medicines etc. are cleared away

Norma's case stands in the hall. Mr Wonderful is seated on the couch C, *with the usual expression of ursine angst*

The radio is on in the front room: Peggy Lee singing I'm a Woman

Norma enters from the kitchen, singing along to the song and carrying an opened bottle of chilled Chardonnay. She is dressed for summer, with a touch more style than usual, casual but smart. As she walks towards the front room, the doorbell trills

She goes to it and admits Lazenby

She allows him to kiss her cheek, then leads him into the front room. She puts the bottle on the table next to his mobile phone, then switches the radio off. They stand and regard each other in silence for a moment—Lazenby wary, she quietly confident, subtly changed, resolute

Lazenby Let me say it for you—I'm a neglectful swine.
Norma (*after a pause*) Had hoped I might see you at the funeral. There were only four of us and a dog that wandered in.

Lazenby Desperately wanted to be there, but I've been so tied up—you've no idea.

Norma For a retired divorcee you have quite a social life... (*She sits on the couch*) Sit down if you like, it's——

Lazenby (*cutting in*) Same price as standing. Yes. (*He perches uneasily on the couch,* R *of the bear*)

She regards him for a long moment

Norma (*murmuring*) Mr Wonderful, eh?

Lazenby Not by a long chalk—I'm afraid it was the old "getting in too deep" syndrome again. I am sorry, Norma.

Norma Don't...

He stops and stares. She is looking at the bear

Anyway, I meant him. She wanted him to be buried with her, but in the end I couldn't do it. Couldn't bear the thought of him in the darkness. (*She giggles*) Those bright button eyes staring at nothing. (*She laughs, a shade harshly*) Too soft, that's my trouble. I bet she's furious with me.

Lazenby I don't suppose it matters.

Norma What does matter, Geoff?

Lazenby Sorry?

Norma I said: what does matter?

Lazenby Depends what you mean—not much in the final analysis I suspect. In the grand scheme of things.

Norma There you go then. I knew you'd say that.

Lazenby Well, pick your philosophy—certain great thinkers will tell you nothing matters in the long run, or the short run, come to that.

Norma There you go, then.

Lazenby Others will assert with equal conviction that life is real, life is earnest—everything matters.

Norma This is it. (*She stares at him, inscrutably, like a pupil no longer impressed with her teacher*) And what do you think, Geoff?

Lazenby I, ehr, suppose I favour a stoical detachment, you might say—with a tendency towards the "life is earnest" school? I'm definitely for the enhancement of life, not nihilism.

Norma Would you say love matters, Geoff? Does trust count for anything?

Lazenby Of course.

Norma Matters when you mean what you say, then? For instance, would you say that if someone told you they love you they should mean it?

Lazenby Absolutely, good heavens—to say we love when we don't has to be one of the most despicable of human actions.

Norma Not something you'd dream of doing, eh, Geoff?

Pause. He stares at her, on his guard. She smiles

But you never said it, did you? Not in so many words.
Lazenby Why did you ask me here, Norma?

Norma turns away to the table and pours two glasses of wine. She hands him one

Norma I wanted to be sure. I wanted to look into your eyes one more time.
Mother wasn't so daft... (*She controls herself*)

He sips his drink warily. She puts hers down, gets up and picks up the mobile phone

Lazenby Oh, my mobile. Of course...
Norma Your gizmo. Fascinating, you were right. I've been using it, hope
you don't mind—my relatives in Australia didn't get to the funeral so it was
good to talk.

Pause

She prowls to the door and back with the phone

Become quite attached to it. Seem to have done nothing but wander round
the house with it when I'm not at work.
Lazenby Can I have it back?

In a kind of intense reverie, Norma moves closer, behind him

Norma (*murmuring*) Mother's note said: "Wolf! Wolf! Tia Maria'd but bear
bears all". Mr Wonderful was sitting on this, (*she indicates the mobile*) so
she knew. (*She stoops and speaks close to Lazenby's ear*) What a harem!
Not fussy, are you?
Lazenby Yes, all right, Norma. (*Without looking back, he holds up a hand*)
My property—if you don't mind?
Norma Pretty please—close your eyes and say "Pretty please"...
Lazenby Can we just stop mucking about...?
Norma (*moving back to face him*) Mucking about? That's not a very
scholarly expression, Mr Wolf—in fact, it's downright common. It's
something I might say is that.

Pause

Close your eyes and say "Pretty please" and I'll put it in your hand.

Lazenby sighs with boredom, closes his eyes

Lazenby (*flatly*) Pretty please.

With her back to the audience, Norma picks up the end of the handcuffs not attached to the arm of the couch and snaps them shut around his wrist at the same time as she gives him the mobile. He jerks his eyes open

What the hell are you doing?

Norma steps back and regards him with folded arms, smiling, smouldering

Norma (*laughing*) I'm arresting you, Geoff.

Lazenby Give me the key, Norma.

Norma (*tossing the key away*) There you go—you're here to answer some serious charges, cock—and I use that word advisedly. You're here to help me with my enquiries.

Lazenby Into what might I ask?

Norma grabs the mobile back

Norma This! Your voice mailbox of silly old tarts, lonely Lils, bimbos—and *nice* trusting women—intelligent women! Your willing witless ladies in waiting!

Lazenby "Willing"—you said it, Norma.

Norma Some of 'em make me ashamed of my own sex. Never thought of myself as prudish, but some things should be done behind closed doors with the wardrobe up against it, don't you think? All this full-frontal stuff... I'm not sure it "enhances life" that much. Was it all that sex? Did it send you a bit crazy?

Lazenby Release me and I'll be on my way, Norma? (*He sips his drink unfazed, almost nonchalant*) Let's just leave it, eh? No names, no packdrill...

She leans over him, shaking the mobile phone

Norma There are twenty women on this thing! Twenty stupid bitches like me! I want to know why you do it.

He just regards her with a supercilious smile. She controls herself and speaks close to his face

I knew there'd be wolves on the dating agency scene—Christ, I've met some. But you... I was almost in love with you.

Lazenby Almost?

She stares at him and takes the hurt on the chin

Norma All right, you shit—was... (*She thinks*) Am... I thought I was untouchable as well as untouched, but you tapped me. You broke my shell just like that... (*She clicks her fingers in his face, then draws the mobile back*) I could smash your face.

Lazenby That's not you, Norma, let me go.

Norma You had us eating out of your hand. Pity the technology let you down—how far were you going to take me before you made your excuses and left?

He shrugs. She stands back slightly and regards him

Said you'd "knocked around the Med a bit" in the Navy, Geoff. Did you get to Turkey?

Lazenby Let—me—go.

Norma I'm going thisaft. Mother didn't leave much, not enough to save me from the card factory—so I thought: have a month off, Norma love, get your naughty bits brown and give the mirror a thrill when you get back.

Lazenby Your mother said you were disturbed.

Norma 'Course I am! Tate and Lyle! Mad Axe Virgin, that's me. Like the outfit? (*She does a little twirl in front of him*) I'm going to have a ball—or maybe two if a nice Turkish waiter comes along! (*She laughs at his expression*) Hate it when I'm crude, don't you? I saw that early on—sort of enjoyed shocking you a bit. Now it puzzles me. A ruthless shag-nasty who's squeamish about language...? (*She sighs*) And I thought you were a gentleman.

Lazenby You're no lady.

Norma *Careful*—I'm sensitive and I've got you handcuffed to a couch they had to bring in through the window... A month's a long time.

Lazenby Oh, cut the crap.

Norma (*smiling*) Don't worry, I've made arrangements for your food. Don't want Rolf Harris putting you on the box emaciated. (*She gets a bag from behind the door and scatters the contents on the floor: bone-shaped dog biscuits*) Not what a wolf's used to, I know, but you'll get to like 'em.

Lazenby Stop being absurd, what do you want?

Norma Why do you do it?

Pause

Why?

Pause

Why?

Pause

*Suddenly he thrashes against the chain, trying to break it and growling with
fury. He is both childish and chilling. Norma is shocked at this glimpse of his
real self. She stares as he stops, panting*

No. You don't like being tied, do you? You've got a savage heart.

Their eyes meet and lock

Lazenby Stop it now, free me.
Norma How did it start? Did you look in the shaving mirror one morning
and see a cruel face...? Teeth getting longer, sharper? (*She checks her
watch*) Tell me! My flight's at two o'clock.
Lazenby There was nothing to it—it was simple!

*She strolls behind the couch again and he strains uneasily to keep her in sight,
then gives up*

Norma Like falling off a log.
Lazenby Yes! One thing led to another! I didn't set out to be a... (*He stops*)
Norma (*close to his ear*) Wolf wolf wolf.
Lazenby Look. I liked you, Norma, you were different.
Norma Mm—don't suppose there are that many forty-something virgins
around. (*She thinks*) Plenty of middle-aged women who wish they'd
stayed one maybe.
Lazenby It wasn't that—you made me laugh.
Norma Want to be my agent? I do impressions as well... (*She stops
clowning. Coldly*) Tell me the truth. I need to understand this.
Lazenby All right! I started dating like you did, like anyone does—hope
springs eternal and all that—sex-starved. You know what I mean?

She nods

Half a dozen women down the line, I realized. Most were pathetic, many
were available. But I'm a bit like you.

She shakes her head

Oh yes, I didn't want it on a plate—not after the first hunger was assuaged
anyway. It became a game, an adult amusement—my recreation. You
know how long I'd been married, Norma!

Pause

She moves slowly back to the front of the couch

Twenty-five years with a woman who wouldn't make love with the light on, then suddenly…

Norma Bimbos galore!

Lazenby Women… Of all ages. I love sex, Norma, I can't get enough—you know that. Every time so different, so new. Such variety, Norma. Oh, I've heard ignorant men say women are all the same, but I've never thought that. It's in the details, you see? And it's the details which lead you on—to obsession, to love if you're not careful. So alluring—a particular cast of face, a way of walking or talking or both—a voice which makes you go weak at the knees. I worship the female if you must know—in her infinite *variety* I adore her.

Norma As long as she's not a permanent fixture.

Lazenby (*scoffing, bitter*) I've had a permanent fixture, Norma! I've spent half my life, my best years waiting for some wonderful fulfilment which didn't happen. I've been there, done it—got the bloody scars.

Norma You're addicted, Mr Wolf.

Lazenby I won't stop, I can tell you that. I live in a world I never knew existed—a sensual world, Norma. Every woman I lie with makes me young again for a while—makes me stop thinking about death. And I've got the best of it—I've got that first glowing romantic bit over and over again. I never get bored. Two months is about average from first date to… (*He stops*)

Norma The drop?

Lazenby I never let it start to die. I'm cruel to be kind.

Norma It doesn't have to die, doesn't have to be like that.

Lazenby Speaking from your vast experience, Norma? Your *True Love* library books?

He laughs at her expression

Norma (*hit but defiant*) There's someone for me somewhere.

Lazenby Grow up, Norma? There's no Mr Wonderful—*I know*.

She is stunned by his certainty

That's what I use, you fool! That romantic crap is my stock in trade—it hardly ever fails. It's the easiest thing in the world to make woman's eyes light up with: "I love you". (*He smiles at her, not without compassion*) I didn't even have to say it to you. I sensed that you didn't like men who come on too strong. I could tell you have imagination—and the imaginative ones do it to themselves: give a little, take a little, make 'em laugh— (*he smiles fondly*) or let 'em make you—brighten up their dull life, then go away a little to let the contrast show. Let the darkness back in. Be honest, Norma— you did it to yourself?

Norma (*hit*) Why did you come back?

Lazenby (*shrugging*) Mobile.

Norma That all?

Lazenby Had you, hadn't I? Case closed.

Norma hits rock bottom. He smiles at her impotence. She dredges herself back up to meet his towering condescension

Norma You cynical using bastard.

He nods

You're the one who needs to grow up—you're nothing but a greedy little boy let loose in a sweet shop.

Lazenby (*laughing*) Too true! Cherry Lips! Pick'n'Mix! Lickerarse allsorts—I love 'em all!

Norma You don't know what love is—there's more to it than screwing around!

Lazenby Listen to you, Norma Green—"Miss Solitary Screw 1998"!

He laughs then stops laughing as she picks up the bear and heads for the door

Norma Toodle-oo.

Lazenby Come off it, Norma…

She stops between the couch and the door

We both know you're not going to leave me alone—you're not the type.

Norma You're right, of course. (*She moves* c *with the bear in her arms*) Anyway, I can't hate you somehow—I've learnt from you. I've been doing it wrong; it's no good looking for someone else to save your life—only you can do that cos only you's living it—excuse the grammar. So… (*She waltzes the bear gently around*) I'm gonna look for myself first, try to love myself a bit, as Richard and Judy might say—then maybe someone will stumble into my tent one night.

Lazenby On a package holiday?

Norma You're such a snob, I'm gonna get rat-arsed and dance under the olive and walnut trees… My own dance. (*She stops abruptly and heads for the door*)

Lazenby You can't leave me alone.

Norma (*in the doorway*) You're not going to be alone, but Mr Wonderful's coming with me, not keen on parties.

Lazenby Parties?

Norma Not party animals, you might say—but I know you love company, so—enjoy!

Lazenby What are you talking about? I don't want to go to a party or anything else—let me go at once!

Norma But all your friends are coming, Geoff. (*She glances at the mobile on the table*) I've arranged the biggest date of all time for you—on your gizmo. Bugger the expense, eh?

Lazenby What?

Norma All your girlfriends are due here at… (*She checks her watch, grinning*) Any minute.

Lazenby (*calling her bluff*) They wouldn't come for you! You couldn't get them to come.

Norma (*in posh Queen Mum voice*) "Ew hellew, this is Geoffrey's Auntie speaking." (*She changes to a younger affected voice*) "Hellew, this is Trish, Mr Lazenby's PA—you dewn't know me but I'm calling to say"…

Lazenby What the hell did you tell them?

Norma (*briskly*) That you need help and to come straight in as you're in bed with gonads like light bulbs after your vasectomy went septic—OK, cock?

Lazenby You're bloody barking! I thought you were nuts on the first date and I was bang-on! If anything untoward happens to me, I'll have the law on you, you hear?

Norma Interpol… And the RSPCA. (*She smiles with bewildering sweetness at Lazenby and goes out into the hallway. She picks up her case*)

Lazenby Norma… Norma, this is silly.

Norma goes out of the front door, case in hand and bear on hip, leaving the door ajar. She laughs as she goes

Norma…

Pause

The Light changes slightly, ageing. Lazenby is slumped on the couch, diminished, fatigued. He looks towards the door at the sound of light footsteps on the path or pavement outside. Someone knocks on the door

A gaggle of women approach on stabbing high heels. Someone rings the silly bell. A woman giggles off, another laughs more roundly

Woman (*off; clearly*) Who are you, then?

Others (*off*) Who am I? Who are you? Would you mind getting out of the way? Geoff? Geoffrey?

The women's voices build into that of a feminine Tupperware party cum lynch mob. The Light goes down slowly on Lazenby's increasing trepidation, anxiety, fear, horror. The voices build

Women (*off*) Geoffrey darling? Geoff? Geoffrey? (*Then stop*)

Peggy Lee starts to sing Mr Wonderful, *continuing*

Black-out

FURNITURE AND PROPERTY LIST

Further dressing may be added at the director's discretion

ACT I

SCENE 1

On stage: **Lop Wink**'s mountain bike on blocks (present throughout)

        MANCHESTER PUB:
        Dado rail and wallpaper painted on flats
        Repro table. *On it*: ashtray, Boddingtons beermats
        2 chairs
        Toilet sign on wall

Set: Drinks on table, empty tonic bottles
        Norma's handbag

Personal: **Norma:** wrist-watch (worn throughout)

SCENE 2

On stage: GREEN'S HOUSE:
        Hallway:
        Side table. *On it*: telephone
        Mirror

        Front Room:
        Couch with wooden arms
        Tiled fireplace
        Cheap ornaments on mantel
        Print on wall

        Phoebe's Room:
        Old brass bed with feather mattress, covers, pillows
        Chamber pot under bed

Zimmer frame
Teddy bear
Knitting
Women's magazines including *Hello*
Tray with liquorice allsorts
Small portable TV set
Books about the Royal Family
Bedside locker with medicines, water jug, glass
Framed photo of Queen Mother, picture of Royal Family, photo of
   Norma, photo of **Phoebe**, photo of Arthur Green
Side table
Hand mirror
Newspaper
Electric socket

Off stage: Handbag (**Norma**)

SCENE 3

On stage: GREEN'S HOUSE

SCENE 4

On stage: MANCHESTER PUB

Set: Glasses
   Norma's handbag

Personal: **Wink**: cycling helmet, gloves (worn throughout)
   Lazenby: wrist-watch (worn throughout)

SCENE 5

On stage: GREEN'S HOUSE

Set: Police issue handcuffs

Off stage: Hoover (**Norma**)

SCENE 6

On stage: MANCHESTER PUB

Set: Drinks

SCENE 7

On stage: GREEN'S HOUSE

Set: Comb
         Tissue

Off stage: Tea-service and sandwiches on tray (**Norma**)
         Flowers, box of liquorice allsorts (**Lazenby**)
         Teapot (**Norma**)

ACT II

SCENE 1

On stage: MANCHESTER PUB

Set: Empty glass
         Folded newspaper

SCENE 2

On stage: GREEN'S HOUSE

Set: Knitting

Off stage: Big box of liquorice allsorts (**Lazenby**)

SCENE 3

On stage: As before

Set: Expensive suitcase in hallway
         Bottle of Tia Maria

Off stage: Cheaper, smaller suitcase (**Norma**)

Personal: **Lazenby:** flash new mobile phone

SCENE 4

On stage: As before

Set: Glass of Tia Maria
            Bottle of Tia Maria on table

SCENE 5

On stage: SOUTHPORT HOTEL:
            Flats
            Table. *On it*: tray with cafetière, two coffee cups, cup of sugar cubes
            Small table. *On it*: bills
            Phone on wall

Off stage: Slip of paper (**Waiter**)
            Financial Times (**Lazenby**)

SCENE 6

On stage: GREEN'S HOUSE

Set: Tousled sheets
            Teddy bear

Off stage: Cases (**Lazenby**)

SCENE 7

On stage: As before

Re-set: **Phoebe**'s bed, stripped to ticking mattress and piled pillows

Set: **Norma**'s case in hall
            Teddy bear on couch
            Lazenby's mobile phone on table
            2 glasses
            Handcuffs attached to arm of couch, with key
            Bag of bone-shaped dog biscuits behind door

Off stage: Bottle of Chardonnay (**Norma**)

LIGHTING PLOT

Property fittings required: nil
3 interior settings.

ACT I, SCENE 1

To open: General pub lighting

Cue 1   **Box**: "Screwdrivers."   (Page 4)
           Black-out

ACT I, SCENE 2

To open: Evening lighting in sitting-room

Cue 2   **Norma** switches light on in hallway   (Page 5)
           Bring up lights in hallway

Cue 3   **Phoebe** stares down at **Norma**   (Page 10)
           Black-out

ACT I, SCENE 3

To open: Early evening glow in sitting-room

Cue 4   **Phoebe**: "Oouuh! I say…"   (Page 15)
           Black-out

ACT I, SCENE 4

To open: General pub lighting

Cue 5   **Norma**: "There you go, then…"   (Page 22)
           Black-out, spotlight on **Lop Wink**

ACT I, Scene 5

To open: Morning lighting in sitting-room

Cue 6   **Phoebe**: "He'll never ring…"   (Page 26)
             Black-out, strobe of moonlight on **Lop Wink**

ACT I, Scene 6

To open: General pub lighting

Cue 7   **Norma** and **Lazenby** stare at each other   (Page 30)
             Black-out, spotlight on **Lop Wink**

ACT I, Scene 7

To open: Early evening lighting in sitting-room

Cue 8   **Norma** folds her arms resignedly   (Page 36)
             Fade lights down, to spotlight on **Lop Wink**, *then
                 bring lights up when ready*

Cue 9   **Norma** stares down at **Phoebe**   (Page 40)
             Slowly decrease lighting to focus on bed

Cue 10   **Norma**: "Mother."   (Page 40)
             Black-out

ACT II, Scene 1

To open: General pub lighting

Cue 11   **Norma** stares straight ahead   (Page 44)
             Slowly fade lights down

ACT II, Scene 2

To open: Flickering TV effect in sitting-room

Cue 12	**Norma** switches TV off	(Page 44)
	Cut TV effect	

Cue 13	**Phoebe**: "Norma!"	(Page 50)
	Black-out	

ACT II, Scene 3

To open: Mid-afternoon lighting in sitting-room

Cue 14	Sound of car starting and leaving	(Page 54)
	Change lighting to golden, tarnishing, darkening,	
	closing in on bed, then black-out	

ACT II, Scene 4

To open: Muted TV flickering effect in sitting-room

Cue 15	**Phoebe** tuts and shakes her head	(Page 56)
	Focus lighting on bed	

Cue 16	**Phoebe**: "Norma!"	(Page 56)
	Black-out	

ACT II, Scene 5

To open: Morning lighting in hotel

Cue 17	**Lazenby** comforts **Norma**	(Page 59)
	Black-out	

ACT II, Scene 6

To open: Mid-morning sunlight in sitting-room

Cue 18	**Norma** reveals mobile phone	(Page 61)
	Black-out	

ACT II, SCENE 7

To open:	General lighting in **Norma**'s house	
Cue 19	**Lazenby**: "Norma..."	(Page 69)
	After pause, change lighting slightly, ageing	
Cue 20	**Women**'s voices build up	(Page 70)
	Fade lights down slowly on **Lazenby**	
Cue 21	Peggy Lee starts to sing *Mr Wonderful*	(Page 70)
	Black-out	

EFFECTS PLOT

ACT I

ACT II

Cue 25   **Norma** nods and is still for a moment   (Page 59)
               Increase volume of seagulls slightly, harsher

Cue 26   Black-out   (Page 59)
               Peggy Lee sings He's a Tramp

Cue 27   Black-out   (Page 61)
               After a moment, Peggy Lee sings I'm a Woman

Cue 28   To open Scene 7   (Page 61)
               Radio on in front room: Peggy Lee singing I'm a Woman

Cue 29   **Norma** walks towards front room   (Page 61)
               Front doorbell trills

Cue 30   **Norma** switches radio off   (Page 61)
               Cut radio music

Cue 31   Someone knocks on front door   (Page 69)
               *Sound of women approaching on high heels, doorbell
                 ringing, woman giggling, another laughing more
                 roundly, their voices building as script page 70,
                 then stopping, ending with Peggy Lee singing*
                 Mr Wonderful, *continuing*